Student Success Manual

to accompany

Understanding Human Communication

Student Success Manual

to accompany

Understanding Human Communication
Eleventh Edition

Ronald B. Adler
Santa Barbara City College

George Rodman
Brooklyn College, City University of New York

Prepared by
Dan Rogers

New York   Oxford
Oxford University Press

Oxford University Press, Inc., publishes works that further Oxford University's
objective of excellence in research, scholarship, and education.

Oxford   New York
Auckland   Cape Town   Dar es Salaam   Hong Kong   Karachi
Kuala Lumpur   Madrid   Melbourne   Mexico City   Nairobi
New Delhi   Shanghai   Taipei   Toronto

With offices in
Argentina   Austria   Brazil   Chile   Czech Republic   France   Greece
Guatemala   Hungary   Italy   Japan   Poland   Portugal   Singapore
South Korea   Switzerland   Thailand   Turkey   Ukraine   Vietnam

Copyright © 2012 by Oxford University Press, Inc.

Published by Oxford University Press, Inc.
198 Madison Avenue, New York, New York 10016
http://www.oup.com

Oxford is a registered trademark of Oxford University Press

ISBN 978-0-19-978200-0

Printing number: 9 8 7 6 5 4 3 2 1

Printed in the United States of America
on acid-free paper.

Contents

Contents

INTRODUCTION

LEARNING STYLES

People learn in different ways. Some understand best by reading (and rereading), while others prefer listening to explanations. Still others get the most insight from hands-on experiences. Knowing your preferred way to take in and learn information can contribute to your college success. You might prefer to see information, to hear information, or to work with information in a hands-on way. In college you won't always be able to choose how information comes to you. Professors require lectures, textbooks, essays, labs, videos, and readings. In this section we'll help you understand your preferred learning style and help you discover ways to approach your studies that will work best for you.

In the next few pages we introduce five learning preferences and provide the opportunity for you to identify your own preference. Then you can put that information to work for you. There are many approaches to learning styles and preferences; here we present one of them, VARK, an acronym for Visual, Aural, Read/Write, and Kinesthetic ways of learning. A fifth category, multimodal, recognizes learners who have two or more strong preferences. No approach is better or worse than others; this is an opportunity to identify your learning preference and use that information to facilitate your college success.

The best way to begin is to identify your learning preference. You can do this by completing the following questionnaire.

The VARK Questionnaire

This questionnaire aims to find out something about your preferences for working with information. You will have a preferred learning style, and one part of that learning style is your preference for the intake and output of ideas and information.

Choose the answer that best explains your preference and circle the letter next to it. Please circle more than one if a single answer does not match your perception. Leave blank any question that does not apply, but try to give an answer for at least ten of the thirteen questions.

When you have completed the questionnaire, use the marking guide to find your score for each of the categories, Visual, Aural, Read/Write, and Kinesthetic. Then, to calculate your preference, use the scoring chart.

1. You are about to give directions to a person who is standing with you. She is staying in a hotel in town and wants to visit your house later. She has a rental car. You would

   a. draw a map on paper.
   b. tell her the directions.
   c. write down the directions (without a map).
   d. collect her from the hotel in your car.

2. You are not sure if a word should be spelled "dependent" or "dependant." You would

   a. look it up in the dictionary.
   b. see the word in your mind and choose by the way it looks.
   c. sound it out in your mind.
   d. write both versions down on paper and choose one.

3. You have just received a copy of your itinerary for a world trip. This is of interest to a friend. You would

   a. phone her immediately and tell her about it.
   b. send her a copy of the printed itinerary.
   c. show her on a map of the world.
   d. share what you plan to do at each place you visit.

4. You are going to cook something as a special treat for your family. You would

   a. cook something familiar without the need for instructions.
   b. thumb through the cookbook looking for ideas from the pictures.
   c. refer to a specific cookbook that has a good recipe.

5. A group of tourists has been assigned to you to find out about wildlife reserves or parks. You would

   a. drive them to a wildlife reserve or park.
   b. show them slides and photographs.
   c. give them pamphlets or a book on wildlife reserves or parks.
   d. give them a talk on wildlife reserves or parks.

6. You are about to purchase a new stereo. Other than price, what would most influence your decision?

   a. the salesperson telling you what you want to know
   b. reading the details about it
   c. playing with the controls and listening to it
   d. it looks really smart and fashionable

7. Recall a time in your life when you learned how to do something like playing a new board game. Try to avoid choosing a very physical skill, like riding a bike. You learned best by means of

   a. visual clues—pictures, diagrams, charts.
   b. written instructions.
   c. listening to somebody explaining it.
   d. doing it or trying it.

8. You have an eye problem. You would prefer the doctor to

   a. tell you what is wrong.
   b. show you a diagram of what is wrong.
   c. use a model to show you what is wrong.

9. You are about to learn to use a new program on a computer. You would

    a. sit down at the keyboard and begin to experiment with the program's features.
    b. read the manual that comes with the program.
    c. telephone a friend and ask questions about it.

10. You are staying in a hotel and have a rental car. You would like to visit friends whose address/location you do not know. You would like them to

    a. draw you a map on paper.
    b. tell you the directions.
    c. write down the directions (without a map).
    d. collect you from the hotel in their car.

11. Apart from the price, what would most influence your decision to buy a particular book?

    a. You have read it before.
    b. A friend talked about it.
    c. You quickly read parts of it.
    d. The way it looks is appealing.

12. A new movie has arrived in town. What would most influence your decision to go (or not go)?

    a. You heard a radio review about it.
    b. You read a review about it.
    c. You saw a preview of it.

13. You prefer a lecturer or teacher who likes to use which teaching tools?

    a. a textbook, handouts, readings
    b. flow diagrams, charts, graphs
    c. field trips, labs, practical sessions
    d. discussion, guest speakers

The VARK Questionnaire—Scoring Chart

Use the following scoring chart to find the VARK category that each of your answers corresponds to. Circle the letters that correspond to your answers. For example, if you answered b and c for question 3, circle R and V in the question 3 row.

Question	a category	b category	c category	d category
3	A	R	V	K

Scoring Chart

Question	a category	b category	c category	d category
1	V	A	R	K
2	R	V	A	K
3	A	R	V	K
4	K	V	R	
5	K	V	R	A
6	A	R	K	V
7	V	R	A	K
8	A	V	K	
9	K	R	A	
10	V	A	R	K
11	K	A	R	V
12	A	R	V	
13	R	V	K	A

Calculating Your Scores

Count the number of each of the VARK letters you have circled to get your score for each VARK category.

Total number of **V**s circled =   (Visual score)

Total number of **A**s circled =   (Aural score)

Total number of **R**s circled =   (Read/write score)

Total number of **K**s circled =   (Kinesthetic score)

Calculating Your Preferences

Because you can choose more than one answer for each question, the scoring is complex. It can be likened to a set of four stepping stones across water.

1. Add up your scores: V + A + R + K =   (total)

2. Enter your scores from highest to lowest on the stones in the diagram, with their V, A, R, and K labels.

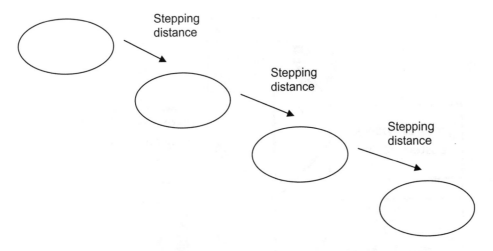

3. Your stepping distance comes from this table.

Total of my four VARK scores is	My stepping distance is
10–16	1
17–22	2
23–26	3
More than 26	4

4. Your first preference is your highest score, so check the first stone as one of your preferences

5. If you can reach the next stone with a step equal to or less than your stepping distance, then check that one too. When you cannot reach the next stone, you have finished defining your set of preferences.

Now that you've scored your questionnaire, find the help sheet in the following pages that matches your preferred learning style. Go to the help sheet for each preference you have checked. If you have more than one preference checked, you should also read the material on multimodal preferences. Look at the specific strategies to study and learn (intake) information during class and independent study and then become familiar with and practice ways that will help you do well on exams (output). Read more about this resource for learning at www.vark-learn.com.

Visual Study Strategies

You want the whole picture, so you are probably holistic rather than reductionist in your approach. You are often swayed by the look of an object. You are interested in color, layout, and design, and you know where you are in your environment. You are probably going to draw something.

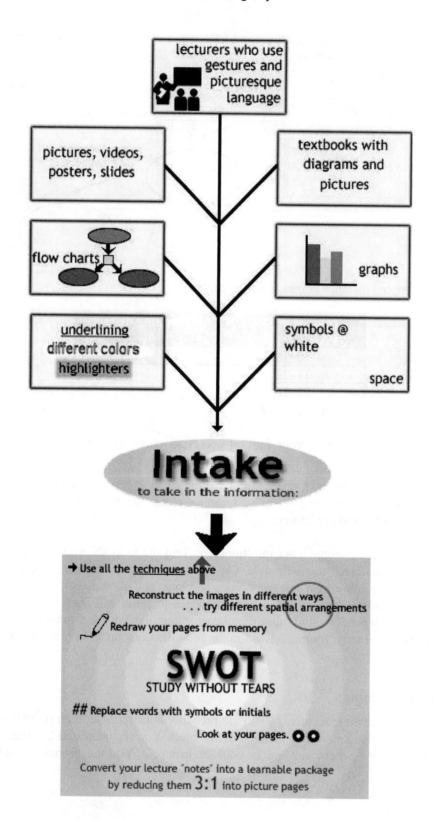

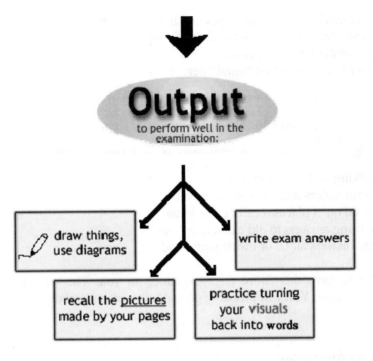

© copyright 2001 Neil Fleming

Aural Study Strategies

If you have a strong preference for learning by aural methods (**A** = hearing), you should use some or all of the following:

INTAKE
To take in the information:

- Attend classes.
- Attend discussions and tutorials.
- Discuss topics with others.
- Discuss topics with your teachers.
- Explain new ideas to other people.
- Use a tape recorder.
- Remember the interesting examples, stories, and jokes.
- Describe the overheads, pictures and other visuals to somebody who was not there.
- Leave spaces in your notes for later recall and "filling."

SWOT—Study without Tears
To make a learnable package:

Convert your notes into a learnable package by reducing them (3:1).

- Your notes may be poor because you prefer to listen. You will need to expand your notes by talking with others and collecting notes from the textbook.

- Put your summarized notes onto tapes and listen to them.
- Ask others to "hear" your understanding of a topic.
- Read your summarized notes aloud.
- Explain your notes to another "aural" person.

> **OUTPUT**
> To perform well in any test, assignment, or examination:

- Imagine talking with the examiner.
- Listen to your voices and write them down.
- Spend time in quiet places recalling the ideas.
- Practice writing answers to old exam questions.
- Speak your answers aloud or inside your head.

You prefer to have this entire page explained to you. The written words are not as valuable as those you hear. You will probably go and tell somebody about this.

Read/Write Study Strategies

If you have a strong preference for learning by reading and writing, you should use some or all of the following:

> **INTAKE**
> To take in the information:

- lists
- headings
- dictionaries
- glossaries
- definitions
- handouts
- textbooks
- readings—library
- notes (often verbatim)
- teachers who use words well and have lots of information in sentences and notes
- essays
- manuals (computing and laboratory)

```
┌─────────────────────────────────────────┐
│        SWOT—Study without Tears          │
│        To make a learnable package:      │
└─────────────────────────────────────────┘
```

Convert your notes into a learnable package by reducing them (3:1).

- Write out the words again and again.
- Read your notes (silently) again and again.
- Rewrite the ideas and principles into other words.
- Organize any diagrams, graphs, figures, or pictures into statements, for example, "The trend is. . . ."
- Turn reactions, actions, diagrams, charts, and flows into words.
- Imagine your lists arranged in multiple-choice questions and distinguish each from each.

```
┌─────────────────────────────────────────┐
│                 OUTPUT                    │
│   To perform well in any test, assignment,│
│             or examination:               │
└─────────────────────────────────────────┘
```

- Write exam answers.
- Practice with multiple-choice questions.
- Write paragraphs, beginnings, and endings.
- Write your lists (a, b, c, d; 1, 2, 3, 4).
- Arrange your words into hierarchies and points.

You like this page because the emphasis is on words and lists. You believe the meanings are within the words, so any talk is okay, but this handout is better. You are heading for the library.

Kinesthetic Study Strategies

If you have a strong kinesthetic preference for learning, you should use some or all of the following:

> **INTAKE**
> To take in the information:

- all your senses—sight, touch, taste, smell, hearing
- laboratories
- field trips
- field tours
- examples of principles
- lecturers who give real-life examples
- applications
- hands-on approaches (computing)
- trial and error
- collections of rock types, plants, shells, grasses, . . .
- exhibits, samples, photographs, . . .
- recipes—solutions to problems, previous exam papers

> **SWOT—Study without Tears**
> To make a learnable package:

Convert your notes into a learnable package by reducing them (3:1).

- Your lecture notes may be poor because the topics were not "concrete" or "relevant."
- You will remember the "real" things that happened.
- Put plenty of examples into your summary. Use case studies and applications to help with principles and abstract concepts.
- Talk about your notes with another kinesthetic person.
- Use pictures and photographs that illustrate an idea.
- Go back to the laboratory or your lab manual.
- Recall the experiments, field trips, and so on.

> **OUTPUT**
> To perform well in any test, assignment,
> or examination:

- Write practice answers and paragraphs.
- Role-play the exam situation in your own room.

You want to experience the exam so that you can understand it. The ideas on this page are valuable only to the extent that they sound practical, real, and relevant to you. You need to do things to understand.

Multimodal Study Strategies

If you have multiple preferences, you are in the majority, as somewhere between 50 and 70 percent of any population seems to fit into that group.

Multiple preferences are interesting and quite varied. For example, you may have two strong preferences, such as VA or RK, or you may have three strong preferences, such as VAR or ARK. Some people have no particular strong preferences, and their scores are almost even for all four modes. For example, one student had scores of $V = 9$, $A = 9$, $R = 9$, and $K = 9$. She said that she adapted to the mode being used or requested. If the teacher or supervisor preferred a written mode, she simply used that mode for her responses and for her learning.

So, multiple preferences give you choices of two, three, or four modes to use for your interaction with others. Some people have admitted that if they want to be annoying, they stay in a mode different from the person with whom they are working. For example, they may ask for written evidence in an argument, knowing that the other person much prefers to refer only to oral information. Positive reactions mean that those with multimodal preferences choose to match or align their mode to the significant others around them.

If you have two dominant or equal preferences, please read the study strategies that apply to your two choices. If you have three or four preferences, read the three or four lists that apply. You will need to read two, three, or four lists of strategies. People with multimodal preferences will use more than one strategy for learning and communicating. They feel insecure with only one. Alternatively, those with a single preference often "get it" by using the set of strategies that aligns with their single preference.

There seem to be some differences among those who are multimodal, especially those who have chosen fewer than seventeen options. If you have chosen fewer than seventeen of the options in the questionnaire, you may prefer to see your highest score as your main preference—almost like a single preference. You are probably more decisive than those who have chosen seventeen-plus options.

Summary of VARK Scores

Now that you are familiar with your preferred learning style, come back to these pages and review the activities that will help you learn and process information best. Your favorite learning style may not match the teaching style used by the professor in this course. If that's the case, take the initiative to learn the material in the other ways outlined for you in the preceding pages while you continue to develop your ability to learn in ways that aren't your favored method.

Based on what you learned about your preferred learning method, list five specific things you can do to help yourself learn the material in this communication course.

1.

2.

3.

4

5.

STUDY SKILLS

Academic success doesn't just depend on how smart you are or how hard you work: it also depends on how *well* you study. Many students spend hours with their books but don't manage to understand the material they're expected to know. Not all methods of "spending time" with the text are equally productive, so we present here several methods that can help you study effectively.

Use SQ3R

SQ3R is a widely used acronym for an effective method to study a text. The method includes these five steps:

S—Survey
Q—Question
R—Read
R—Recite
R—Review

Survey

Begin by getting an overview of the material you'll later study in detail. Start with one chapter. Look at the title of the chapter and the major headings. Survey the opening page with its Chapter Highlights and objectives. Skim the chapter's tables, photos, cartoons, sidebars, figures, charts, and summaries. Glance at the Critical Thinking Probes and Ethical Challenges. At the end of each chapter, peruse the Key Terms, Activities, and Resources. This big-picture survey will help you put each section of the chapter in a larger context.

Question

Go back over the headings you have just surveyed and turn each one into a question. Most questions will include one of the following words: who, what, when, where, how, or why. Look how topics from *Understanding Human Communication* can fit into these forms:

- Who has power in groups? (Power in Groups, Chapter 9)
- What are the ways to help others when they have problems? (Empathic Listening, Chapter 5)
- When should you reveal personal information, and when should you keep it to yourself? (Guidelines to Appropriate Self-Disclosure, Chapter 7)
- Where can you find information for your speech? (Gathering Information, Chapter 11)
- How can you paraphrase? (Informational Listening, Chapter 5)
- Why is misunderstanding so common? (The Language of Misunderstandings, Chapter 4)

Read

Once you've reworded each section as a question, you can read the material to find an answer. Read only one section at a time, to make sure you understand it before going on. As you answer a question, don't just rely on material in the text. Think about what you already know from your life experiences and from other classes.

Consider reading in a way that takes advantage of your strongest learning style. If your learning style is visual, highlight as you read, and translate what you read into pictures, drawings, and diagrams in the margins or in your notes. If your learning style is aural, consider reading the book aloud, taping it, and then listening to the tape. If you learn best by reading/writing, you'll want to read all of the handouts and practice questions provided. If you're a kinesthetic learner, you'll learn by doing the activities on the course website and completing the exercises at the end of each chapter. Review the specific strategies for your learning style presented in the preceding pages and use them.

Recite

After you've read the material, test your understanding by putting the ideas into your own words. Another word for reciting is *explaining*. Your goal here is to test your knowledge by rewording it. You can do this either in writing or by verbally explaining the material to a study partner, friend, or family member.

Reciting takes many forms; in fact, you'd be wise to use as many senses as you can. Consider using the techniques you learned in the VARK analysis. Are there some methods that work particularly well for your learning style? Now is the time to use them. If you're a visual learner, look up from your reading and recite what you've just learned by picturing the answer. Recall a visual from your notes and turn it into words. If you're an aural learner, speak your knowledge aloud and hear it in your own voice. If your preferred learning style is reading/writing, write the answer in your own words and read it in your own handwriting. If you are a kinesthetic learner, try to use all of your senses. Think of real-life experiences and examples of what you're learning; act out concepts by actually practicing the skills in this course in various real situations. Most important in this step is translating information into your own words, not just memorizing someone else's words.

Review

Finally, review what you've learned by creating summarizing statements—either in full sentences or in outlines. You can create review documents in short chunks (e.g., sections of a chapter) or on a chapter-by-chapter basis. These review documents can serve you well as you study for exams, so be sure to save them.

SQ3R is not a method to speed up studying like speed-reading techniques, and it is not a method for cramming the night before a final. It is a long-range approach to better understanding and retaining knowledge learned over the course of the semester. It is a method for studying texts that can help you succeed in this course if applied early and consistently. Learning in small segments and reviewing often results in greater learning and retention than cramming. We have inserted reminders to use this method in each chapter of this *Student Success Manual*.

Additional Study Ideas

Mark Your Texts

Forget the admonitions from your elementary teachers not to mark in your books. Studying is not a passive activity. You want to do more than just read your text; you want to study it, prepare for your exam, and increase your long-term retention of the information. When you mark your text you involve touch and movement, not just vision. This increased activity can stimulate brain activity and aid recall. Writing side notes to yourself, underlining, circling, and highlighting involve you in the process of learning. Here are some guidelines for marking your texts:

1. **Read before you mark.** To be able to figure out what is most important, you need to read a paragraph or section before you mark it up. As you read, try to distinguish main points from details. Analyze as you read to see categories and relationships of ideas. Before you mark, determine what is most important to focus on in order to review and remember.

2. **Develop a code of your own.** You might use circles for thesis statements and underlining for examples. When subpoints are spread out over several pages, you might use one color to highlight items of the same category. Use brackets, parentheses, underlining, or quotation marks; develop a system that works for you. Improve your ability to spot the key ideas, relationships, causes and effects, and contrasts and similarities. If you need to, write down your code at the beginning of the chapter.

3. **Make notes in the margin.** Summarize a section in a few words of your own. Translate information into your way of talking and relate it to the lecture, another class, or your personal life. Create a short outline or drawing in the margin to help you recall or relate information. Annotate for your benefit—do what helps you.

4. **Mark thoughtfully; don't just mark everything.** Marking more than 20 percent of the text defeats the purpose of distinguishing the key information to review later. Read first and think carefully about what to mark.

Choose Your Environment

Choose an effective setting in which to study. A successful study setting has minimal interruptions and distractions from external noise, other people, phones, televisions, and doorbells. Using a computer may help you take notes, organize your information, create study guides, and focus on the material you're learning, or it might distract you with e-mail, instant messages, and the temptation to surf. It will take resolve not to answer the phone or check e-mail during your study time. Think about the physical environment of your study location and its comfort in terms of furnishings, lighting, and temperature. Consider furniture that is comfortable but will not lull you to sleep. Chairs, desks, and lighting should give you space and motivation to read and write. Keep the resources you need (paper, pencils, highlighters, dictionary) but not a lot more. Once you have identified a place that works well for you to study, train yourself to use that place often so your brain associates serious study with that location. College libraries usually have well-designed, well-lit spaces with minimal distractions. The Study Environment Analysis (www.ucc.vt.edu/stdysk/ studydis.html) allows you to analyze study settings to determine the best environment for you.

Attend Study Sessions

If your professor or TA announces a study session, make it a priority to attend. These small sessions provide opportunities to review and ask questions. If your professor does not sponsor study sessions, form a study group with other dedicated students. Talking through the material, reviewing each other's notes, and quizzing each other will enhance your study skills and your comprehension and retention of the course concepts.

Seek Help

Familiarize yourself with your campus tutoring centers and labs, study skills workshops, student success centers, communication labs, supplemental instruction, peer mentoring, learning support services, learning assistance centers, or student learning centers. Check out resources to assist you in studying, writing assignments, and preparing for exams.

If you have a learning difficulty or disability, locate and use available services. The Office of Student Services (or the Office of Special Services) provides screening, diagnosing, and assistance for students with learning difficulties or special needs. If you already have documentation of a special need, take that to the appropriate office to receive services more quickly. If you think you may have dyslexia, attention deficit/hyperactivity disorder (ADHD), or any learning disability, you can arrange for a professional screening. After the screening, you can be referred for further testing or to other services to meet your needs. To those who ask, colleges usually provide note takers, books on tape, additional time for tests, and other reasonable accommodations for special needs.

Taking Notes in Class

The preceding section offered advice for studying on your own. This section will help you understand the material that your professor presents in class. In addition to using the approaches for class lectures, you can use them as a supplement or alternative to the SQ3R approach for better understanding the text and other readings. Two popular methods of note taking are the Cornell format and mind maps.

Cornell Note-Taking System

Taking notes while reading or while listening to a lecture occupies much of your time as a student. One tried-and-true method of note taking is the Cornell system. You can utilize this system with the following steps:

1. Before you begin to take notes, draw a vertical line down the left side of your paper about a fourth of the way over (2 inches from the left on an 8½ × 11 inch page).

2. As you listen for main points (see Chapter 5's section on informational listening), take notes on the right side.

3. Later, as you review your notes, put key words, significant phrases, and sample questions in the left column.

SAMPLE: Cornell Note-Taking System

2. Second, pull out key words and phrases and create questions here.	1. First, take notes on this side. Leave space to add to notes from text or readings. Focus on big ideas.
Group Interdependent What size is a small group?	Groups are collections of individuals that interact over time and are interdependent. Usually between 3 and 20 people.
Hidden agenda	Group members have common goals. Individual goals not shared with the group are called hidden agendas. (One person wants to make connections to get a new job—something just for him—but the group goal is to complete a report.)

Mind Mapping

Mind mapping is a technique you can use to take notes from a lecture or text and improve your recall of the ideas. A mind map is a visual representation of the material that emphasizes relationships of concepts. While an outline emphasizes linear relationships, a mind map (also called a concept map) shows associations, links and connections in a holistic way. An outline is more like a book; a mind map resembles information assembled as Web links. Visual learners especially benefit from this method.

To construct your mind map, follow these guidelines:

1. Start in the middle of a large unlined sheet of paper.

2. Use only key words, not sentences.

3. Use images (arrows, circles, sketches) that help you recall ideas and show relationships between words and groups of words.

4. Use colors to link related ideas and separate others.

5. Be creative.

A mind map of a lecture on listening might look like this:

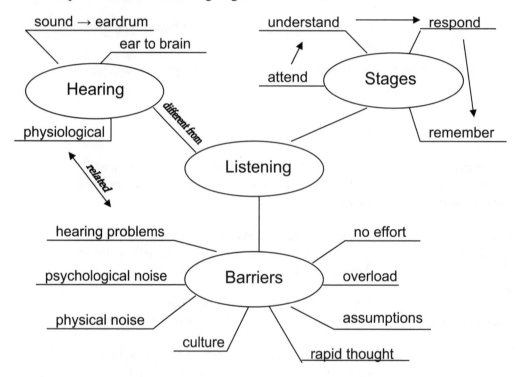

TEST-TAKING SKILLS

In most of your classes, you will take exams. Whether these are short, five-question quizzes or two-hour essay exams, the following tips can help you improve your exam scores.

1. **Prepare for the exam you'll be given.** Read the syllabus carefully or talk with your instructor to find out what types of exams you'll take. Your text, this *Student Success Manual*, and the *Understanding Human Communication* website provide many tools to study for different kinds of exams. Ideally, you'll know the material well enough to be able to pass any type of exam; practically, you can use your time and energy to prepare most efficiently if you know the type of exam you'll be faced with. Here are some pointers for three common types of exam questions.

True/False

A. If the *whole* sentence isn't true, it isn't true. Conversely, if any part is false, it is false. Don't be thrown off by a partial truth buried in an otherwise false statement. Look for any falsehood.

B. Be aware of absolutes (always, never, only) and remember that if there is one exception, the question is false.

C. Statements phrased with negatives can be confusing. If changing it to a positive makes it true, the original sentence phrased as a negative is generally false. For example, "Nonverbal communication cannot be used to deceive." If you make this sentence a positive, it becomes "Nonverbal communication can be used to deceive." Since this is true, the opposite of the sentence must be false.

Multiple Choice

A. Read the first part of the question and think of the answer you would give if no choices were provided. Then see if that is one of the choices.

B. Before marking the answer, read all the choices to be sure yours is the best. Most multiple-choice directions say choose the **best** answer; so all choices may be somewhat correct, but one might be superior to the others. For instance, if you are choosing the best paraphrase, and one choice paraphrases only thoughts and another choice paraphrases only feelings, look for a *best* answer that paraphrases both thoughts and feelings. If one choice is more complete than others, it may be the best choice, even though others may be technically correct, as well.

C. Check if "all (or none) of the above" is a choice. If you know for sure that two or three choices are correct (or incorrect), consider the "all (none) of the above" option.

D. Negative questions can be confusing. If the question is worded as a negative, look at each option and mentally change the question to a positive. Then mark each choice that works. Generally, you will mark all but one, and that one will be the correct answer for the original (negative) question. For example, "Which of the following is **not** a function of nonverbal communication?" can be mentally changed to "Which of these **is** a function of nonverbal communication?" If all but one choice correctly answers the second question, the unmarked question will generally be your answer to the original question.

E. If two choices seem too similar to permit a distinction, reread the question to be sure you understand what is being asked. Check carefully for some small difference in the answers, making one a better choice. Perhaps neither is correct; see if there is a better answer altogether.

Essay

A. Familiarize yourself with the types of words used in essays and be sure you understand their meaning. Commonly used words are *describe, review, explain, compare, contrast, discuss,* and *evaluate*. For each word, the instructor looks for a different reasoning process and type of answer. Read the question carefully and mark the words that tell you what type of answer is expected. Familiarize yourself with the definitions of twenty commonly used words found in essay questions at http://www.studygs.net/essayterms.htm

B. Create an initial outline for each answer. Jot down an outline for each question, organizing your ideas around major themes that answer the question. State your thesis and your support. While you are writing one answer, if an idea pops into your head for another question, quickly add it to the outline.

C. Divide your time so that you will be able to answer each question. Your professor may give you partial credit for an outline or some sentences that show you understand the material, even if the grammar isn't correct and the thoughts aren't complete. Leaving a 10-point question blank results in losing 10 points, no matter how extensive your answer to another question is.

D. Write neatly, leaving space between your lines. This will allow you to go back and add information you think of later. If you are writing and you know the concept but can't think of the precise term or name, leave a blank, describe it, and fill the blank in later. You may think of the term or name as you proceed, or it may be used in another part of the exam.

2. **Predict and prepare for likely types of test questions.** Use the outline provided in this *Student Success Manual* and the more extensive one in the *Study Guide* on the course website to predict objective questions. For instance, if there are four steps or three characteristics listed, be prepared for a multiple-choice question that asks, "Which one of these is . . ." or "Which one of these is not. . . ." Creating an outline or mind map from your lecture notes will help you predict questions on that material.

3. **Use practice questions effectively**. Use the course website to practice multiple-choice, true/false, fill-in-the-blank, and matching questions. Use this *Student Success Manual* to study for short-answer and synthesis questions. When you use sample questions with an answer key, don't look at the answer key while answering the questions. If you simply tell yourself (after seeing the correct answer), "Yes, that's the answer I would have chosen," using the sample exams will not benefit you. Take the sample exams as actual exams without looking at the answers. Then go back and grade yourself. Doing this will reveal gaps in your knowledge and help redirect your study time more productively.

4. **Arrive rested, early, and relaxed**. Be sure you've slept and eaten. Be comfortable and settled before the exam is handed out, with any necessary pens, pencils, and blue books at hand. Put away any unnecessary items so you're not distracted. If you can, relax your body by taking a few slow, deep breaths. Anxiety produces a body on "alert" that is not as capable of test taking as a calmer body.

5. **Plan your time.** Know how much each section of the exam is worth and then set up a time frame for yourself so you'll be able to spend the appropriate amount of time on each section. Check your time to be sure you're staying on task. If there is no penalty for guessing, then guess.

6. **Begin with what you know**. Peruse the exam and jot down ideas for questions you'll answer later. Then begin with the easy questions first to build confidence and get in the swing of things.

7. **Use the hints the exam provides.** Read carefully. Often the answer to one question is contained in another question. Stay alert to information that might be given. If one question is "List and describe the twelve major categories of Jack Gibb's theory of supportive and defensive communication" and another question is "Jack Gibb is best known for his theory of _____," the answer to the second is contained in the first.

8. **Analyze your exam to prepare for the next one.** Always learn from one exam so you can improve on the next one. An exam analysis is provided on the next page. Complete the exam analysis before you talk with your instructor and take it with you; it shows that you are serious about learning from exams, not just grubbing for points.

Postexam Analysis

After your exam, go through the exam and note the number of each item you missed, the code for the type of question you missed, the code for the reason you missed it, and any additional information that is important.

Come up with a plan to improve your studying and your exam scores.

Code for types of questions missed:		
MC = Multiple Choice	**T/F** = True, False	**SA** = Short Answer
E = Essay	**FB** = Fill in the Blank	**M** = Matching

Code for reasons I missed items:
AB = Absent the day it was covered.
NN = Not in my notes, although I was in class and took notes when the item was explained.
N = It was in my notes, but I didn't study or comprehend it.
T = Answer was in the text; I didn't read it or didn't remember it.
MRQ = I misread the question. (reading error)
MUQ = I read the question but misunderstood what was asked. (comprehension error)
V = I didn't understand some of the general vocabulary used to ask the question.
DRC = I didn't read all choices; I picked one I thought was right without reading all.
H = I hurried to get to the end.
RCW = I had it right, erased it, and changed it to a wrong answer.

# Exam question missed	Code for type of question	Code for reason I missed the question	Additional, important information about the question or answer

Now go through your columns and see if you can determine a pattern. Did you miss mostly one type of question? Seek help for answering that type of question. Did you miss questions for one particular reason? What can you do to rectify that?

Write a paragraph in which you summarize what you learn from this analysis and create, in list or paragraph format, a plan to improve the skills you need to do better on the next exam.

WRITING

In addition to study and test-taking skills, your grades in college often hinge on your writing assignments. You've been learning to write for years, and in college it is especially important to apply all you've learned. Successful writing depends on your planning, development, organization, avoidance of plagiarism, and mastery of writing mechanics.

Planning

Read the assignment carefully and ask about anything you don't understand. Underline words on the assignment sheet that give requirements or planning details. Know how long the paper is supposed to be. Begin by clarifying your purpose so you know exactly why you are writing and who your audience is. Understand whether you are being asked to express an opinion, prove a point, analyze a situation, synthesize research, apply a theory, summarize an article, or accomplish some other purpose. Personal response or application papers are very different from book summaries, abstracts, or research papers. Determine whether your paper will be read only by your professor, by a panel, or by classmates as well. If you know your purpose and your audience at the outset, you can plan more successfully. Write down your audience and purpose, and then sketch out a tentative thesis, outline, and possible supporting materials. See the step-by-step advice for planning major papers in "Timeline for a Term Paper" at the end of this section.

Development

Short opinion or analysis papers may not require outside research. They will, however, require that you develop your thoughts and support for your ideas carefully, but not necessarily with outside research. You will improve your development of any paper if you clarify your understanding of the types, functions, and styles of support explained in Chapter 12 of *Understanding Human Communication* ("Supporting Material"). While the activities of writing and speaking differ, the underlying principles and guidelines will serve you well in developing the types of support most appropriate to your paper. Whether you need to check a few facts or conduct extensive research, "Gathering Information" in Chapter 11 will help you develop your paper by using search engines, evaluating websites, and conducting library research.

Organization

Whether preparing papers or speeches, you'll do well to follow the guidelines for organization presented in Chapter 12 of *Understanding Human Communication*. Start with a thesis statement and carefully organize your main points and subpoints in a logical pattern. (See "Principles of Outlining" and "Organizing Your Points in a Logical Order.") Then structure your supporting material coherently for greatest impact. Use transitions in your paper as you would in a speech, to help readers understand the direction of your paper and how what you've already said relates to what comes next. (See "Using Transitions.") Finally, when your paper is largely written and you see your creation as a whole, it is time to write an introductory paragraph that gets the readers' attention, states the thesis, and previews the main points. Then write your conclusion so it reviews your thesis and main points and creates closure. Looking at the introduction and conclusion side by side helps you see whether your paper has unity and cohesion. (See "Beginning and Ending the Speech.")

Plagiarism

Virtually every student knows that cheating is a grave academic offense. Nobody who copies answers from a stolen test or a friend can claim ignorance of the rules as a defense. Plagiarism, though, isn't as well understood. Read your college's code of conduct or code of academic integrity to see its definition of academic dishonesty and plagiarism. Here is a breakdown of the most widely recognized types of plagiarism.

Copying

Replicating another person's work word for word is plagiarism. This includes any format or activity that involves taking someone else's work (e.g., a paper, speech, cartoon, or exam) and presenting it as your own in any form (report, speech, or paper). If you are quoting someone else directly in writing, indicate the person's words in quotation marks and properly cite the source. A handbook of English usage will show you how to do citations. In speaking, use an oral citation to clarify the words and the source. Sometimes, plagiarism results from hurried or careless research. If you later cannot determine whether your note cards contain a summary in your own words or quotations from your source, your work may contain plagiarism. Avoid this risk by consistently using quotation marks appropriately and carefully coding your notes.

Paraphrasing

Even if you put others' writings in your own words, you must credit the source. If the words are largely your own paraphrase, but include key words and phrases from another source, put the key words and phrases in quotation marks and cite the source.

Using Ideas

Even though you are not quoting or paraphrasing, credit the source of an idea. The exception is information that is common knowledge and is found without credits in multiple sources of high quality. For instance, almost all communication texts list many types of nonverbal communication, including a category about how far or close we are when we interact with each other. The existence of this category, called proxemics, is common knowledge and needs no citations. However, if you describe the distances at which we interact as "intimate, personal, social, and public," those are the words and ideas of Edward T. Hall, and his work would need to be cited.[1]

---

[1] E. Hall, *The Hidden Dimension* (Garden City, NY: Anchor Books, 1969).

Drawing on Nonprint Sources

The basis of your writing might be a movie, television show, radio broadcast, or website. If ideas, paraphrases, or quotations come from these, be sure to cite them. Style guides and English usage handbooks give you formats for doing so.

In brief, credit those who shape your research and ideas. In the process, your citations demonstrate that you've researched and studied beyond your text. You get credit for researching and also enhance your credibility when you cite quality work. Be sure to do your own synthesizing, analyzing, and reflecting on your research so that your thesis and writing reflect your own thinking and your paper is not just a series of quotations strung together. The ideas, organization, and particular process of asking and answering a research question should be yours. Demonstrate that you have original thoughts, interpretations, analyses, and means of expression supported by current research and experts.

Grammar and Mechanics

No matter how brilliant your thoughts are, grammatical and mechanical errors create "noise" for the grader, causing your ideas to get lost. Use complete sentences to create coherent paragraphs. A spelling and grammar check on your computer helps, but it misses errors of many types, so don't rely solely on it. Use the online and in-person resources available to you to review grammar and spelling concerns. After you proofread, have a tutor or competent friend read your paper to see if it makes sense, is readable, and is free of errors. Double-check that your paper adheres to specific requirements with regard to acceptable font style and size, spacing, margins, and style (APA or MLA).

Checklist for Your Paper

Reviewing this checklist might improve your paper and your grade. Does your paper:

☐ get your readers' attention in the opening paragraph?

☐ state your thesis and preview your main points in your opening paragraph?

☐ present ideas in an organized and logical manner?

☐ sound coherent? Do ideas make sense and hang together?

☐ have a topic sentence in each paragraph and other complete sentences that logically follow to make a point?

☐ develop ideas with adequate support for the points made?

☐ use transitions to help the reader understand the movement from one idea to another?

☐ have an interesting and summative conclusion that reviews the main points and brings closure?

☐ use the required sources (kind and number)?

☐ cite all sources in the proper style?

☐ mark direct quotations appropriately?

☐ credit paraphrases and ideas of others?

☐ have no spelling and grammar errors?

☐ include a cover page (if required) with title, your name, professor's name, course number and section, and date?

☐ conform to the deadline?

☐ adhere to requirements for length, spacing, fonts, and any additional instructions on the assignment sheet?

Timeline for a Term Paper

Postponing a writing assignment is a plan for disaster. It's not likely that you will be able to put together a decent paper if you start a day or two before the deadline. Use a calendar or day planner to plot the day the assignment is due and then work backward to design a workable timeline of activities needed to complete the paper. For a term paper, create a semester plan. Adjust your timetable accordingly for shorter writing assignments that may not require as much research. Always allow time to revise and rewrite. The Assignment Calculator (www.lib.umn.edu/help/calculator) prompts you to plug in the date your paper is due and displays a day-planner guide to work on this assignment. Each step of the way you can click on tools to help you organize your thoughts, create a plan, and locate detailed tips.

As you proceed, save your work frequently, and always make a copy of your work so you never lose all of it. Too many students have learned this lesson the hard way with a low grade to prove it.

For a research paper due the 14th week of the term, your timeline might look like this:

Weeks 2–3

✓ **Know your assignment**. Read the assignment carefully and ask questions if you are not sure what the process and the final product should look like.

✓ **Update your research skills**. Students are often unaware of the resources in their university library. What resources—journals, books, databases, special collections—do you have access to? Don't think you have to discover these on your own: get to know the reference librarian and ask for help.

✓ **Choose your topic.** If the professor is assigning topics, get yours as early as you can. If there is a list to choose from, pick yours early. If the topic is your choice, make sure your instructor agrees that it fits the assignment. See Chapter 11 of *Understanding Human Communication* for advice on choosing a topic. When you've identified a likely topic, do a quick search to see if there seems to be enough information. Narrow your topic. Make sure it can be covered properly in a paper of the length assigned for the project.

Weeks 4–5

✓ **Develop a research question** that specifically asks the question you are trying to answer through your research. Careful wording of the question helps you organize and plan your research and, later, your writing.

✓ **Clarify the kinds of research required**. Professors may allow only scholarly (peer-reviewed) journals or may require a certain number or percentage be scholarly. The number and type of websites allowed may be limited. Know before you begin so you use your time wisely.

✓ **Devise your research strategy** by working with a reference librarian to find the information you need. Ask about indexes, catalogs, databases, and Internet resources. Keep records of the sources (databases, key words, websites) you've researched so you don't duplicate your efforts.

✓ **Critically review and evaluate your sources**. See Web references in the Internet Resources section to help you with this.

✓ **Take notes and create a working outline.** Careful notes help you avoid plagiarism and clarify what is or isn't another person's work. Be consistent with a system to indicate whether you have exact quotes, paraphrases, or ideas from another person.

✓ **Record your sources in the required format** so that you can properly cite them in your references or works-cited list. Know what style is required for your final paper and cite your sources in that format now. This will save hours of backtracking later to find a part of the citation you'd forgotten. Most communication courses will use APA or MLA styles; references for both are in the Internet Resources section beginning on page 33.

✓ **Broaden or narrow your topic** depending on the amount of information you find.

Weeks 7–9

✓ **Create a thesis statement and outline.** When you have much of the information you need, develop a thesis and main points in complete sentences, and note where your research will be inserted to develop your points. Your outline helps you see what pieces of information are missing and what sections require more research.

✓ **Continue your research** to round out your paper.

Weeks 10–11

✓ **Begin writing** when you have all of your information and your outline. As you write, focus on answering your research question.

✓ **Follow the technical requirements** for the paper. Read the assignment or check with the professor to be certain about the spacing, font size, margins, style (APA or MLA), and cover required.

✓ **Revise and rewrite.** Allow time to seek help from your professor, TA, writing lab, or tutor. Be certain to print a hard copy and create a backup of everything at this point. Back up your work each time you revise.

Weeks 12–13

✓ **Proofread**. Ask others to read your paper for coherence and to spot any errors.

✓ **Finish** your paper at least two days before the due date to allow for computer crashes and printer problems. Print a copy and proofread the hard copy. This also guarantees having something in hand, should you experience a technology failure.

CLASSROOM CIVILITY

You'll be more successful in this and other classes if you accept the responsibilities that come with being a student.

1. **Know the rules of the course.** Check your syllabus; it generally spells out what you can expect in the class and what's expected of you. Since no two classes have identical rules, you can save yourself grief and boost the odds of success by investing time in reading the syllabus for every class. Some professors even give a pop quiz on the contents of the syllabus.

2. **Attend each class.** Attendance plays an important part in college success, and students who don't skip class have several advantages: they hear explanations of assignments and changes in assignments, due dates, or test dates. They hear test reviews, they can ask questions, and they often gain an edge if a grade is borderline. Attendance attests to your seriousness as a student and your willingness to take responsibility for your learning. In a communication class such as this, participation in class activities often accounts for learning the skills and is part of the assessment (grade) for the course, as well.

3. **Show up on time**. In some cultures and some high schools, being tardy is accepted, but the culture of college classrooms is that classes start on time and you're tardy (or marked absent) if you're not there for the start of class.

4. **Come prepared**. Check the syllabus and be sure you read the assigned chapters before class. You'll be prepared for quizzes, activities based on the reading, and lectures. You'll also understand more from the lectures.

5. **Accept responsibility: What you do (and don't do).** If you're absent from a class, find out what you missed from your professor or other students before the next meeting and do what's necessary to stay caught up. If the syllabus clearly tells you to check the website and not to contact the professor to find out what you've missed, follow that advice. Turn in work on time. If an assignment is late, acknowledge that fact. Excuses usually won't impress your professor, who has probably heard them all before.

   Another way to accept responsibility is to avoid the "you" language described in Chapter 8. For example, instead of attacking your professor by saying, "You didn't explain this very well," use "I" language and say, "I didn't understand. . . ."

6. **Behave in a civil manner.** Since you don't want to antagonize your professor and fellow students, follow the basic rules of civil behavior in groups. Show up on time to class. Turn off your cell phone and pager. Don't hold side conversations or butt into a lecture or discussion without being recognized first.

7. **Show your interest.** Even if you aren't constantly fascinated by what's happening in class, acting the part of an interested student will make a good impression; and often acting interested may even help you feel more engaged. Nonverbal indicators that you are interested include leaning forward, making eye contact, smiling, nodding responsively and appropriately, asking sincere and thoughtful questions, and volunteering for activities if

asked. These behaviors will likely enhance your own learning and that of your classmates. In addition, you will help to create a supportive classroom climate.

Ask questions. If you don't understand, ask. Ask in a way that does not create defensiveness or take unnecessary class time. If something has been explained, try to identify the specific point you don't understand, rather than ask for the whole topic to be repeated. Specific questions, such as asking the professor to differentiate between two points, "Could you explain when self-concept and self-esteem are different?" or asking for an example, "Could you give an example of how self-concept and self-esteem differ?" will help you more than a general request like, "Can you go over self-concept and self-esteem again?" As you study, prepare questions that delve deeper into the material, questions that will help you understand. If you feel uncomfortable or if there is no opportunity to ask in class, try to ask the professor after class, during office hours, or by e-mail. The important thing is to ask.

Avoid behaviors that say you're *not* interested in class: text-messaging, reading another book, talking, rummaging through your pack or purse, putting your head down, sleeping, and so forth. You get the picture.

8. **Treat others with respect in class discussions.** Listen to other points of view. Part of classroom civility is hearing and responding appropriately to others' opinions. Classrooms are marketplaces of ideas; prepare to hear and listen to opinions different from yours.

Understand others before responding. Before you respond to someone else, be sure you've understood his or her point of view. Use perception checks (Chapter 3) and paraphrases (Chapter 5) to clarify what the other has said before you respond. Use these skills to ensure that you don't embarrass yourself with a lengthy disagreement, only to find that you had misunderstood the point.

In your own comments, avoid acting dogmatic when you are actually expressing your opinion. Rather than saying, "Women are . . ." or "Men are . . .," use the phrase, "In my opinion, women are . . ." or "In my experience, men are. . . ." This shows that you understand the difference between facts, opinions, and inferences—concepts covered in Chapter 4. Other phrases that can help you be clear about recognizing that what you are saying is your own opinion, not absolute fact, are "I have learned . . . ," "I have come to believe . . . ," "I am convinced . . . ," or "I have concluded. . . ." This sort of language is less likely to trigger defensiveness than dogmatic statements. You can help reduce defensiveness and build a positive communication climate (Chapter 8).

9. **Stay positive**. Approach the class with a positive attitude, and never take out your frustration on the professor or other students. Stating that you're frustrated is okay but unnecessary. Stating "I want to be sure I understand this" or "I want to learn this" can serve as a positive affirmation for you, your professor, and your classmates. You will generally get a more positive reaction than if you begin on a negative note like, "This is really hard. I don't know how you expect us to remember all these key terms." Focus on your goals. If your goal is to learn and to understand, stay focused on that. For more details about positive thinking benefits for students, see www.marin.cc.ca.us/~don/Study/Hcontents.html.

10. **Recognize that success takes work.** Joining a class is like signing up for a gym membership; even though you're a "customer," you will benefit only if you follow the plan your coach (i.e., your professor) sets out for you. Commit to showing up for your classes (workouts) ready to do what it takes to tone up your understanding.

How well are you doing? Use the Classroom Savvy Checklist to find out. www.mtsu.edu/~studskl/savylist.htm.

INTERNET RESOURCES

Attention Deficit Disorder

Causes, characteristics, treatment, and legal issues plus strategies for coping, studying, and learning: www.ucc.vt.edu/stdysk/addhandbook.html

Attitude

www.marin.cc.ca.us/~don/Study/Hcontents.html

Avoiding Plagiarism

www.georgetown.edu/honor/plagiarism.html#country
www.indiana.edu/~wts/pamphlets/plagiarism.shtml

Classroom Savvy Checklist

www.mtsu.edu/~studskl/savylist.htm

Cornell Note Taking

www.bucks.edu/~specpop/Cornl-ex.htm

Evaluating Sources

http://owl.english.purdue.edu/workshops/hypertext/EvalSrcW/index.html

Learning Styles

www.vark-learn.com

Marking Texts

http://www.utexas.edu/student/utlc/lrnres/handouts/1420.html

Mind and Concept Mapping

How to mind map with sample: www.mindtools.com/mindmaps.html
How to mind map: www.peterussell.com/MindMaps/HowTo.html
Outline/example of mind mapping: www.bucks.edu/~specpop/sem-map.htm
Examples of web, tree, chart, chain, sketch:
        www.bucks.edu/~specpop/vis-org-ex.htm#web

Concept mapping:
    www.utc.edu/Administration/WalkerTeachingResourceCenter/FacultyDevelopme
    nt/ConceptMapping/index.html#what-is
Concept mapping homepage: http://users.edte.utwente.nl/lanzing/cm_home.htm

Overcoming Procrastination Self-Help Program

http://www.utexas.edu/student/utlc/class/mkg_grd/pselfhelp.html

SQ3R

www.studygs.net/texred2.htm
www.arc.sbc.edu/sq3r.html
www.teach-nology.com/web_tools/graphic_org/sq3r/

Test-Taking Skills

http://www.studygs.net/essayterms.htm

Writing Assistance

www.ucc.vt.edu/stdysk/termpapr.html
http://webster.commnet.edu/mla/index.shtml
http://owl.english.purdue.edu/handouts/index.html

Writing Papers

www.lib.umn.edu/help/calculator

Writing Styles

APA: www.wisc.edu/writetest/Handbook/DocAPAReferences.html
MLA: http://webster.commnet.edu/mla/index.shtml

CHAPTER 1: HUMAN COMMUNICATION: WHAT AND WHY

SQ3R in Action:

Generate an SQ3R chart for this chapter here:
http://www.teach-nology.com/web_tools/graphic_org/sq3r

Survey

Skim the title, Chapter Highlights, objectives ("You should understand" and "You should be able to"), headings, tables, photos, cartoons, figures, charts, and items in the margin. Glance at the titles of the Critical Thinking Probes and Ethical Challenges. At the end of each chapter, look over the list of Key Terms, Activities, and Resources.

Question

Ask yourself questions. What do you know about these topics from your own life experiences and from other classes? Ask these six questions in each section: who, what, when, where, how, and why.

Read

Take one heading at a time and read to find the answers to the questions you've posed.

Recite

In your own words, say the answer aloud and then write it out.

Review

Review each section and then review the whole chapter. This is a good time to use the activities at the end of the chapter and the activities and the sample exam on the course website.

Chapter 1: Outline

(Italicized words are key terms.)

I.   Human *communication* is the process of creating meaning through symbolic interaction.
- A.   Communication is a continuous, ongoing process.
- B.   Communication is symbolic and arbitrary and allows people to think and talk about the past, explain the present, and speculate about the future.

II.   Types of communication include *intrapersonal*, *dyadic* or interpersonal, *small group*, *public*, and *mass*.

III.   Communication is used to satisfy physical, identity, social, and practical needs.

IV.   The communication process can be diagrammed as a *linear* or *transactional* model but transactional is more sophisticated and accurate.
- A.   The linear model (doing communication to another) consists of a *sender encoding* a message through *channels*, despite *noise*, that the *receiver decodes* with the help of fields of shared experiences or *environments*.
- B.   The transactional model (communication done with others) reflects fluid, simultaneous interaction of sending and receiving by *communicators* using *feedback* that can be observed and interpreted.

V.   Effective communicators have *communication competence*.
- A.   Communication competence is defined as the ability to achieve one's goals in a manner that maintains or enhances the relationship.
- B.   Competent communicators realize there is no one ideal way to communicate. Relationships and environments affect competent communication as a process through trial-and-error and observation.
- C.   Competent communicators choose from a repertoire of a wide range of behaviors and options; the communicator selects the most appropriate behavior with empathy and an appreciation of the other's perspective by constructing a variety of frameworks for viewing an issue.

VI.   Ethical, knowledgeable communicators recognize common misconceptions.
- A.   Communication does not require complete understanding, nor does it solve all problems.
- B.   Communication itself is neither good nor bad; this is because the meaning or interpretation rests in people, not words.
- C.   Communication is not simple, and more is not always better.

Chapter 1: Summary

Defining communication is not simple; but since the text is about understanding human communication, the starting place is to study communication that is unique to members of our species. This ongoing process uses interpretation and past experiences to assign meaning. Rather than static isolated acts, communication unfolds continuously from a series of interrelated symbols and behaviors.

Human communication can occur in many contexts, including internally to self (intrapersonal) or between two people (dyadic). Interpersonal communication is dyadic in nature but with unique qualities that will be explained further in Chapter 7. Human communication also occurs in small groups, whether in person or via mediated channels. Small groups, while a common fixture of everyday life, possess multiple characteristics not present in dyads. Groups are such an important communication setting that Chapters 9 and 10 focus exclusively on them. The procedure of public communication occurs when a group becomes too large for all members to contribute. One characteristic is an unequal amount of speaking with limited verbal feedback. Public communication, being personal in nature, is in a category separate from mass communication. In mass communication, messages are aimed at a large audience without personal contact between sender and receivers.

Perhaps the strongest argument for studying communication is its central role in our lives. Through communication, humans satisfy their physical needs. Communication is the way we acquire our sense of identity. We decide who we are based on how others react to us. Communication provides a vital link to satisfying our social needs. Communication is used for pleasure, affection, inclusion, escape, relaxation, and control. Notice that it would be impossible to fulfill these social needs without communicating with others. And we should not overlook the use of communication to accomplish everyday important practical needs, from giving directions to the hair stylist to explaining the broken pipe problem to the plumber. Communication is a tool deemed an important key in employment, relationships, education, and a variety of everyday situations.

Until recently communication was viewed as something one person "does" to another. This linear model of injecting communication consisted of a sender encoding ideas and feelings and sending the message via communication channels to a receiver, who then decoded the meaning and interpretation. For most people the communication channel of face-to-face contact is the most familiar and obvious. Writing or communicating through some sort of medium such as text messages, e-mail, faxes, instant messaging, Twitter, or blogs has gained prominence in recent years. Any interference that disrupts the effective delivery of the message from sender to receiver is called noise. Noise can occur at every stage of the communication process. There are three types of noise: external, physiological, and psychological. Because senders and receivers often have differing fields of experience, not only of a physical locale but also of personal and cultural backgrounds, the differing environments make understanding others challenging.

A more accurate way to look at communication is that it is "with" others and not "done to" others. This is the transactional model, according to which sending and receiving are treated as simultaneous. Thus the "communicators" are capable of receiving, decoding, and responding to another's behavior, while at the same time that other person is receiving and responding. The discernible response of a receiver to a sender's message is called feedback. Feedback does not have to be verbal and very often the lack of feedback, a nonresponse, can be symbolic in meaning. The "act" of communication cannot be isolated to a discrete precise static event. Communication is fluid and relational. What precedes and what follows affects the message depending on the involvement and interaction of the communication partner.

Recognizing good communicators is easy, and it is even easier to spot poor communicators. But what makes an effective, competent communicator? Communication competence is the process of achieving one's goals in a manner that, ideally, maintains or enhances the relationship in which it occurs. A competent communicator realizes there is no one ideal way to communicate. What is effective in one relationship won't necessarily be competent in others. It is possible to develop communication skills through the process of trial and error and through observation. We learn from our successes and failures. A competent communicator will utilize a large communication repertoire with a wide range of behaviors, choosing the most appropriate behavior after considering the context, the goal, and the other person. Having the ability to recognize and perform the most appropriate way to communicate by means of considering the other person's point of view is an important skill. The value of taking the other's perspective suggests one reason why listening is so important. Being able to combine and construct a variety of frameworks for viewing an issue reflects cognitive complexity. This characteristic allows us to make sense of people by using a variety of perspectives, which in turn leads to a greater "conversational sensitivity" that increases the chances of acting in ways that will produce satisfying results. When paying close attention to one's behavior and using these observations to do the job effectively, one has to care. A strong feature that distinguishes effective communication in almost any context is commitment.

Having spent time talking about what communication is, we ought to also identify some things it is not. Most people operate on the implicit but flawed assumption that the goal of all communication is to maximize understanding. This is a misconception. So is the refrain that communicating clearly is a guaranteed panacea capable of solving all problems. Communication is not always a good thing. The value comes from the way it is used. Communication can be a tool for expressing warm feelings and useful facts, but it can also by used to inflict emotional pain. The ambiguity of language and nonverbal signals offers differing interpretations depending on the communicators involved rather than the actual words themselves. Communication is not simple. Even the best communicators suffer from the frustration of being unable to get the message across effectively. Too much communication is often a mistake. More is not always better. Excessive communication can be unproductive. And there are times when communicating too much can aggravate a problem.

These fundamentals of communication form the foundation for more complex concepts presented in the next chapters.

Chapter 1: Key Terms

For each of these terms, define the term, give an example, and explain the significance of the term.

1. channel

2. communication

3. communication competence

4. coordination

5. decoding

6. dyad

7. dyadic communication

8. encoding

9. environment

10. feedback

11. interpersonal communication

12. intrapersonal communication

13. linear communication model

14. mass communication

15. mediated communication

16. message

17. noise

18. public communication

19. receiver

20. sender

21. small-group communication

22. social media

23. symbol

24. transactional communication model

Chapter 1: Review Questions

These questions are designed to help you understand this chapter's concepts and express your understanding in your own words. For practice with true/false and multiple- choice questions, use the course website.

1.   Define communication and identify the key characteristics of communication.

2.   Give an example of the types of communication identified in this chapter.

3.   Cite the needs satisfied by communication and give an example of each.

4.   Explain the linear model of communication and state clearly why the transactional model is more accurate.

5.   What are the characteristics of a competent communicator?

6.   Identify the common misconceptions about communication.

7.   Human communication is said to be symbolic. Why?

_____ A particular word means the same thing to any two people.

_____ Animals have no appreciation of sarcasm.

_____ Words are arbitrary and open to individual interpretation.

_____ Cultural differences should have no bearing on interpretations.

_____ Machines cannot decode irony.

8.   You are sitting through a long lecture and really need to use the restroom.
The professor poses a question over something just covered but you have no memory of what was said. How can you explain this lapse?

_____ If the speaker had more charisma, you would have known the answer.

_____ Listener etiquette dictates that you acknowledge the teacher's superiority.

_____ There were not enough visual aids to hold your attention.

_____ A type of noise has interfered with your receiving the message.

_____ Responsibility for lack of understanding rests on the sender, not the
        receiver.

Chapter 1: Thinking Outside the Box: Synthesizing Your Knowledge

These questions are designed to help you develop the big picture by blending what you've learned in this chapter and elsewhere.

1. Briefly journal a typical day and your use of the types of communication identified in this chapter to satisfy your needs.

2. Recall a challenging situation involving yourself and a retail sales clerk or manager. Referencing what you have read in this chapter, how would you have improved your communication competence?

Chapter 1: Answers to Review Questions

Your answers should include the following points.

1. *Human communication is the process of creating meaning through symbolic interaction. It is a continuous, ongoing process in which we use interpretation and past experiences to assign meaning. Rather than consisting of static, isolated acts, communication unfolds continuously from a series of interrelated symbols and behaviors. Communication is symbolic and arbitrary.*

2. *Intrapersonal: one person communicating internally. For example: what to wear to school as opposed to what to wear to a job interview.*
   Dyadic: two people communicating back and forth, as in a greeting exchanged in a school hallway.
   Small group: three or more people interacting with shared communication: for example, a group of friends deciding what movie to see.
   Public: one person dominating the speaking with limited feedback from the receivers: for example, a teacher delivering a lecture.
   Mass: messages are aimed at a large audience without personal contact between sender and receivers: for example, newspapers, television commercials, billboards, or notices posted on a bulletin board

3. *Physical: being too cold or too hot or being hungry.*
   Identity: how others indicate that you are tall or thin or young or good-looking.
   Social: associating with friends or displaying proper manners.
   Practical: signaling that you are changing lanes on the highway.

4. *Linear models view communication as something one does to another; that is, a sender encodes and sends a message through channels despite noise so that the receiver can decode the message. Transactional models see communication as a shared interaction of the communicators sending and receiving simultaneously. The transactional model acknowledges shared experiences, and what precedes and what follows contribute to the fluid process of communication.*

5. *Communication competence is situational and relational, It can be learned. Competent communication requires the development of a wide range of behaviors with the ability to choose the appropriate behavior while taking into consideration the empathetic perspective of the others involved. The ability to construct a variety of frameworks for viewing the issue is called cognitive complexity. Self-monitoring awareness contributes to competence, provided the communicator is committed to the relationship.*

6. *Communication does not require complete understanding. It will not solve all problems and is not always a good thing. The actual meanings and interpretations of communication rest in people, not in words. Communication is not simple, and communicating is not always better than not communicating.*

7. *Human communication is considered symbolic because words are arbitrary and open to individual interpretation.*

8. *What has happened is a type of noise has interfered with your ability to get the message.*

Chapter 1: Answers to Thinking Outside the Box

1. *Answers will vary widely. Journal entries should include intrapersonal communication. For example, suppose you need to decide whether to wear a jacket or a sweater or a short-sleeve top, not only to cope with appearance and style, thus addressing identity and social needs, but also to compensate for the weather conditions)that is, to address a physical need). Ordering a meal at a fast-food establishment, on the other hand, exhibits dyadic communication and satisfies the physical need of hunger. Moving a chair to sit with friends satisfies a practical and a social need. Listening to a radio or watching television is an example of receiving content from mass communication, while listening to a lecture exemplifies participation in public communication. Students will encounter multiple applications of the communication types while addressing needs over and over throughout the course of the exercise.*

2. *Answers will vary depending on the encounter, but your recollection should recognize that there is room to improve perspective taking. The environment and situation would have flavored the dialogue and influenced the behavior chosen. Reflection usually highlights behavior that, if not inappropriate, could have been handled with more skill. Usually one finds that certain messages could have been presented*

with more empathy, thus enhancing the process of achieving one's goals in a manner that, ideally, maintains or enhances the relationship in which it occurs.

CHAPTER 2: THE CHANGING WORLD OF COMMUNICATION

SQ3R in Action:

Generate an SQ3R chart for this chapter here:
        http://www.teach-nology.com/web_tools/graphic_org/sq3r

Survey

Skim the title, Chapter Highlights, objectives ("You should understand" and "You should be able to"), headings, tables, photos, cartoons, figures, charts, and items in the margin. Glance at the titles of the Critical Thinking Probes and Ethical Challenges. At the end of each chapter, look over the list of Key Terms, Activities, and Resources.

Question

Ask yourself questions. What do you know about these topics from your own life experiences and from other classes? Ask these six questions in each section: who, what, when, where, how, and why.

Read

Take one heading at a time and read to find the answers to the questions you've posed.

Recite

In your own words, say the answer aloud and then write it out.

Review

Review each section and then review the whole chapter. This is a good time to use the activities at the end of each chapter and the activities and the sample exam on the course website. Remember to periodically review the preceding chapter as well.

Chapter 2: Outline

(Italicized words are key terms.)

I.   Changes in communication technology create communication challenges.

    A.   The accelerating pace of communication innovation presents challenges for interpersonal relationships in school, at work, socializing, and even at play.

    B.   Changing demographics of communicators dissolve the old boundaries.

II.   *Culture* shapes communication.

    A.   Culture consists of the language, values, beliefs, traditions, and customs people share and learn.

    B.   *Coculture* perception and *intergroup communication* influence *salience.*

    C.   We identify with *in-groups* and label those we view different as *out-groups;* but it is important to remember that generalizations do not apply to every member of a group.

III. Subtle yet vitally important values and norms shape the way members of a culture communicate.

    A.   *Low-context* and *high-context* cultures differ in communication styles.

    B.   The *individualistic* and *collectivistic* orientations are viewed as representing the most fundamental dimension of cultural differences.

    C.   *Power distance* and *uncertainty avoidance* influences tolerance of ambiguity.

    D.   *Ethnocentrism* leads to *prejudice* and *stereotyping* but can be overcome with open-mindedness.

IV.   The new masspersonal phenomenon combines *social media* with personal reasons for communicating.

    A.   Social media are interactive and are distinguished by user-generated content.

    B.   Mediated communication differs from the face-to-face form through message *richness* and the use of *synchronous* versus *asynchronous* communication.

    C.   Another difference occurs in permanence comparisons. Face-to-face communication is transitory; by contrast, the mediated form is capable of being stored and forwarded.

    D.   We use social media for information, personal relationships, personal identity, and entertainment.

V.   There are guidelines for social media communication competency.

A. Choosing the appropriate channel, face-to-face vs. social media, can make a difference in achieving successful communication.
B. Consider mediated communication etiquette. Be careful, be considerate, and exhibit civility.
C. Be mindful of boundaries. *Disinhibition* can lead to *flaming* and cyberbullying.
D. Be aware of bystanders, and balance mediated communication with face time to avoid depression, loneliness, and social anxiety.
E. To be safe, always assume that mediated messages can and may be seen and heard by unintended recipients.
F. Cell phone conversations and text messaging combined with driving pose physical safety hazards.

Chapter 2: Summary

Today we are equipped with a wide range of communication technologies presenting new communication challenges. The accelerating pace of communication innovation has caused the study of communication to evolve. It now reflects a changing world with a wide range of aspects, including how relationships develop, the nature of social support, the role of emotions, how honesty and deception operate, and how new technologies affect interpersonal relationships. The changing demographics of today's global village means that you meet and communicate with people of diverse backgrounds every day. Socialization in personal life, the workplace, school, and at play via twenty-first century technology has dissolved the boundaries that used to limit communication.

Daily interaction with various cultures creates communication challenges. Culture is defined as the language, values, beliefs, traditions, and customs people share and learn. This definition is not just in reference to nationalities but can also refer to differences within a society. Membership in a coculture, the perception of belonging to a group that is a part of an encompassing culture, can shape unique patterns of communication. Interaction between members of different cocultures is intergroup communication. The weight we attach to cultural characteristics in intergroup communication, the salience, establishes a distinction between "us" and "them." Groups with which we identify are in-groups. Those we view as different are labeled out-groups. Within every culture, members display a wide range of communication styles. It is important to remember that generalizations, even when accurate and helpful, do not apply to every member of a group.

Along with obvious differences, some less visible yet vitally important values and norms shape cultural influences on communication. The set of circumstances surrounding a situation and giving it meaning, its context, can be identified in two distinct ways. Low-context cultures use language primarily to express thoughts, feelings, and ideas as directly as possible. High-context cultures rely heavily on subtle, often nonverbal cues to maintain social harmony. Both can operate within domestic cocultures and both, directness and indirectness of communication, can present challenges. Members of some cultures view their primary responsibility as helping themselves. This individualistic cultural approach differs from the collectivistic cultural idea of loyalty and obligation to an in-group. These contrasting orientations form the most fundamental dimension of cultural differences, which are made apparent in the varying approaches to handling disagreements.

Power distance refers to the extent of the gap between social groups that possess resources and influence and those that don't. Low-power-distance cultures minimize the differences between various social classes. High-power-distance cultures do not support behavior that challenges authority; rather, they value dutiful, submissive, respectful communication approaches. The degree to which members of a culture feel threatened by ambiguous situations and the degree to which they try to avoid them, uncertainty avoidance, is reflected in the way the people communicate. Members who are made uncomfortable by change and are especially concerned with security tend to be intolerant of people who don't fit their definition of the norm. People from cultures unthreatened by change and characterized by social flexibility regarding rules and regulations are able to tolerate uncertainty.

Intercultural communication competence improves with increased contact. However, increased exposure alone is not enough. There must be a genuine desire to know and understand combined with a tolerance for ambiguity. Without an open-minded attitude, a communicator will have trouble interacting competently. Those with an attitude of ethnocentrism—that is, those who think their own culture is superior to others— tend toward prejudice and stereotyping. Scholarship suggests three strategies for moving toward a more mindful, competent style of intercultural communication. Passive observation, active strategies, and self-disclosure are the recommended ways to acquire culture-specific information that leads to competence.

Until recently, the term *media* designated radio, television, and other forms of mass communication. Today's media is not always aimed at mass audiences. The term *masspersonal* describes a Web 2.0 medium shifting from one-way to interaction via social networking, video- and photo-sharing services, and blogs. Social media delivery exhibits an interactive process represented by text messages, Twitter, Facebook. MySpace, e-mails, instant messages, YouTube, streaming video, and user-generated content with a variable size target audience. The boundary between personal and mass media has become fuzzy.

Mediated and face-to-face types of communication contain similar elements, as discussed in Chapter 1; but there are differences. Most mediated communication lacks the message richness of face-to-face. *Richness* is the term used to describe the abundance of nonverbal cues that add clarity to a verbal message. Thus mediated messages are leaner and harder to interpret with confidence. Synchronous communication, like face-to-face or phone conversations, occurs in real time. If there is a time gap between the sending and receiving of a message, the act of communication is defined as asynchronous. This form of communication gives the receiver the options of editing, seeking advice, or not responding at all. Face-to-face is transitory. Texts and video messages sent via hard copy or mediated channels has a permanence that permits storage and forwarding to others.

Who uses social media? A 75 percent majority of teens and adults under age 30 use social networking. By contrast, only 40 percent of surveyed adults over 30 were social networkers. Adults use online Internet options to send e-mails four times as much as teens. What do people do with social media? The uses and gratifications fall into the categories of information, personal relationships, personal identity, and entertainment.

Social media communication competency goes beyond the general rules of Chapter 1. Deciding how the recipient of your message would prefer to receive it, and acting accordingly, can be difficult, making the effort, however, increases the possibility of achieving success. Since there is, in social media, a permanence not present in face-to-face, be careful what you post. Being considerate, respecting others' need for undivided attention, and using a civil tone are important factors in the etiquette of mediated communication. The tendency to transmit messages without considering their consequences is called disinhibition. Research shows that disinhibited behavior occurs most often in social media and less in face-to-face contact. Flaming outbursts and mediated harassment such as cyberbullying can result in dire consequences. Would you deliver the same message to the recipient in person? If the answer is no, then you might want to think before hitting the "send" key.

Competent social media communicators respect private boundaries and are mindful of bystanders. Some things are none of your "business," nor should all social media communications be shared with people you do not know. Using social media technology in public places can be intrusive and offensive. Is there such a thing as too much mediated socializing? The answer appears to be yes. An uneven balance favoring mediated over face-to-face establishes a link to depression, loneliness, and social anxiety.

Careless use of social media heightens safety issues. Always assume that mediated messages are being or may be shared with unintended, uninvited recipients, some of whom you do not know or trust. The physical safety hazards of phone use and texting while driving are well established. Concentration, vision, and reaction time are all diminished to the danger level of intoxication.

The combination of demographic changes in our global village with new communication technologies has expanded the options for communicating; but the greater variety is accompanied by a unique set of challenges and responsibilities. This chapter provides some tools to help you use social media guidelines competently in the quest for intercultural and cocultural communication in contemporary society.

Chapter 2: Key Terms

For each of these terms, define the term, give an example, and explain the significance of the term.

1. asynchronous communication

2. coculture

3. collectivistic culture

4. culture

5. disinhibition
6. ethnocentrism

7. flaming

8. high-context culture

9. in-groups

10. individualistic culture

11. intergroup communication

12. low-context culture

13. out-groups

14. power distance

15. prejudice

16. richness

17. salience

18.   social media

19.   stereotyping

20.   synchronous

21.   uncertainty avoidance

22.   Web 2.0

Chapter 2: Review Questions

These questions are designed to help you understand this chapter's concepts and express your understanding in your own words. For practice with true/false and multiple- choice questions, use the course website.

1. Define the term *culture*, and identify the various cocultural groups to which you belong.

2. Cite the salience you apply to other cultures when identifying the "us" from "them."

3. What are the distinctive cultural values and norms that influence communication challenges?

4. Social media differ from face-to-face communication through three characteristics. Identify each, and compare and contrast them all.

5. What are the uses of social media, and how do people receive gratification
   from them?

6.   Identify the characteristics of social media communication competency.

7.   The accelerating pace of communication innovation is markedly obvious
   between the under-30 and the over-30 age groups. Which answer highlights
   this difference most accurately?

   _____ over 30 use face-to-face for business and social media for fun

   _____ under 30 are distrustful of nonverbal cues highlighting salience

_____ under 30 prefer social networking and texting twice as much

_____ over 30 have established identities and thus are more competent

_____ under 30 think faster and react more quickly to asynchronous messages

8.   Scholarship suggests three strategies for moving toward a more mindful,
    competent style of intercultural communication. What are they?

_____ interruption, interference, and investigation

_____ prejudice, stereotyping, and disinhibition

_____ conformity, compliance, and convenience

_____ passive observation, active strategies, and self-disclosure

_____ ethnocentrism, discrimination, and minority rule

Chapter 2: Thinking Outside the Box: Synthesizing Your Knowledge

These questions are designed to help you develop the big picture by blending what you've learned in this chapter and elsewhere.

1.   Interview someone of a different culture and ask the person to elaborate on the communication differences he or she found confounding and frustrating upon first encountering the values and norms of the current society.

2.   Imagine that you have been assigned the task of setting parameters and guidelines for personal social media etiquette. Detail the dos and don'ts you would like to see your peers follow.

Chapter 2: Answers to Review Questions

Your answers should include the following:

1.   *Culture is defined as the language, values, beliefs, traditions, and customs people share and learn. Your coculture might include age,*

race/ethnicity, sexual orientation, physical disability, language and accent, religion, activity and hobby, education, income, and other markers of membership in a group.

2. *Since salience refers to the weight we attach to cultural characteristics, this answer should include observations and perceptions of what signifies the in-group of your coculture and what identifiers indicate those in the out-group. It might prove interesting and educational to share your answer with others of your coculture. You might discover others have selected different indicators. This could stimulate discussion regarding who is the "us" and what makes up "them."*

3. *Low-context and high-context messages affect both sender and receiver. Context is communication. Whether the communicators place higher value on individualism or collectivism is a fundamental dimension of cultural differences. Communication is different in low- versus high-power-distance societies. What is the attitude of the communicators regarding uncertainty avoidance? This is often reflected in the way messages are sent and received.*

4. *The richness of the message is one difference. One message might be loaded with nonverbal cues as in posture, facial expressions, or tone of voice; in a leaner message, on the other hand where specificity often distorts intended irony and humor. Another important difference is the reaction time between message sent and message received. Face-to-face occurs in real time and thus is said to be synchronous communication. Mediated communication is referred to as asynchronous because there is a time gap between the sending and the responding, if any. Face-to-face is transitory: the only evidence that it took place is mental recall. Mediated communication has permanence, as represented by a hard copy, a file, or the capability of physical storage.*

5. *This answer should include information, personal relationships, personal identity, and entertainment.*

6. *Choosing the best communication channel indicates competency, even if the right choice is uncomfortable for you. Taking care regarding the permanence status of mediated communication. and the possible repercussions of transmitting such a message, is another aspect of competency. So is being mindful of social media etiquette such as respect for others' need for undivided attention, a civil tone, and avoidance of disinhibition, which can lead to flaming and cyberbullying. There should be self-imposed respect for privacy boundaries and restraint in causing bystanders to be your captive*

audence. An unbalanced heavy reliance on mediated communication over face-to-face can have personal detrimental effects.

7.   *The accelerating pace of communication innovation is markedly obvious between people under and over the age of 30. This is highlighted by the finding that those under 30 use social networking and texting nearly twice as frequently as those over 30.*

8.   *The three strategies for moving toward a more mindful, competent style of intercultural communication are passive observation, active strategies, and self-disclosure.*

Chapter 2: Answers to Thinking Outside the Box

1.   *Answers will vary widely, but dialogue that is open and respectful should reveal fascinating intergroup communication with an empathetic perspective of intercultural sensitivity. Values and norms assumed and expected in one culture may bring into question the level of open-mindedness of the other culture. Ideally, this exchange will prompt dialogue to reveal that there is no right or wrong, only difference. Being different is not inferior or superior; rather, it introduces ambiguity.*

2.   *Definitions of rude and inconsiderate mediated communication behavior are personal. Experience and conditioning in social media reflect control of the message, control of the receiver's attention, effectiveness of delivery, and expectations of comprehension and listening. Are there time limits for response time during a texting exchange? Do you have standards for language usage and expressions? Are there certain barricades not to be breached regarding sharing and forwarding? What ethical guidelines do you impose on yourself and expect from others? Do you think these are understood by others? Is communication competence a challenge because individual etiquette varies within your own coculture? All those questions should be answered here.*

CHAPTER 3: THE SELF, PERCEPTION, AND COMMUNICATION

SQ3R in Action:

Generate an SQ3R chart for this chapter here:
http://www.teach-nology.com/web_tools/graphic_org/sq3r

Survey

Skim the title, Chapter Highlights, objectives ("You should understand" and "You should be able to"), headings, tables, photos, cartoons, figures, charts, and items in the margin. Glance at the titles of the Critical Thinking Probes and Ethical Challenges. At the end of each chapter, look over the list of Key Terms, Activities, and Resources.

Question

Ask yourself questions. What do you know about these topics from your own life experiences and from other classes? Ask these six questions in each section: who, what, when, where, how, and why.

Read

Take one heading at a time and read to find the answers to the questions you've posed.

Recite

In your own words, say the answer aloud and then write it out.

Review

Review each section and then review the whole chapter. This is a good time to use the activities at the end of each chapter and the activities and the sample exam on the course website. Remember to periodically review the preceding chapters as well.

Chapter 3: Outline

(Italicized words are key terms.)

I.   The ways in which we perceive ourselves and others shape our communication.
- A.   Our *self-concept* is a set of relatively stable perceptions that each of us holds about ourself.
- B.   The way we think others view us is most important with respect to the opinions of *significant others*.
- C.   Culture shapes our notion of self through language, individualistic patterns versus collectivistic, and context.

II.   Self-concept is a very powerful force; it influences our behavior and that of others.
- A.   When a person's expectation of a certain outcome, and subsequent behavior, increase the likelihood that the outcome will occur, the phenomenon represented is called a *self-fulfilling prophecy*.
- B.   Sometimes one person's expectations govern the actions of another; this is another form of self-fulfilling prophecy.

III.   How we perceive others shapes our interaction with them.
- A.   We make sense of others' behaviors through *selection*, *organization*, and *interpretation*.
- B.   Our degrees of involvement, personal experience, assumptions, expectations, and knowledge of others create an ongoing perception process.
- C.   *Narratives* are the personal stories we and others create to make sense of our personal world.
- D.   Perception checking can help bridge the gap between different narratives.

IV.   When we use attribution, the process of attaching meaning to behavior, we sometimes commit errors that are due to common perceptual tendencies.
- A.   We make snap judgments and judge ourselves more charitably than we judge others.
- B.   We pay more attention to negative impressions than positive ones, and we are often influenced by what is most obvious.
- C.   We cling to first impressions, even if wrong, and tend to assume that others are similar to us.

V.   Overcoming the challenge of differing perceptions is assisted with *empathy*, the ability to re-create another person's perspective.
- A.   The three dimensions of empathy are perspective taking, emotional dimensions, and a genuine concern for the welfare of the other person.
- B.   *Sympathy* differs from empathy in that it involves feeling

compassion for the predicament without the degree of personal identification present in empathy.

VI.   People use communication strategies known as *identity management* to influence how others view them.

    A.   Each of us possesses a *perceived self*, or *face*, and a *presenting self,* also called *facework*.

    B.   We have multiple identities we reveal in a collaborative process, sometimes consciously, sometimes not; but people differ in their degree of identity management.

    C.   We manage our identities to follow social rules, to accomplish personal goals, and to meet our social needs.

    D.   Despite the availability of common nonverbal cues, computer-mediated communication involves identity management with clarity or ambiguity, seriousness or humor, logic or emotion.

VII.   Identity management is not manipulation or phoniness but rather a part of being a competent communicator in choosing the best role for a given situation.

    A.   There is more than one honest way to behave in most circumstances.

    B.   Too much honesty can be inappropriate.

Chapter 3: Summary

Nothing is more fundamental to understanding how we communicate than our sense of self. This self-concept, a relatively stable set of perceptions that each of us holds about our self, includes what we think is unique to us and different from others. A part of self-concept is self-esteem, our feeling of self-worth. We also develop an image of ourselves from the way we think others view us. This reflected appraisal is particularly important when it comes from significant others, people whose opinions we value most. Their impact on our self-concept depends greatly on the social environment affecting interpretation.

Our whole notion of self is shaped by the culture in which we are reared. Language and accent can indicate membership in an 'out-group," thus causing a pressure to assimilate or a refusal to accede to the majority. Individualistic versus collectivist cultural tendencies reflect a different way of viewing one's self. Interpretation of context regarding directness and honesty causes variance in the feeling of pride and self-worth.

Self-concept both shapes much of our communication behavior and is shaped by it. Self-concept is such a force on the personality that it not only determines how we communicate in the present but can actually influence our behavior and that of others in the future. A self-fulfilling prophecy is one that seems to have been achieved because of a person's expectation of a certain outcome, and subsequent behavior favors the occurrence of that outcome. In a second category of self-fulfilling prophecies, one person's expectations govern another's actions. To a great extent, we are what we believe we are.

The ways we employ to perceive others shape our interaction with them. We sort out and make sense of others' behavior in three steps: selection, organization, and interpretation. Once we have developed an organizing scheme to classify people, we use it to make generalizations. Our degree of involvement, relational satisfaction, personal experience, assumptions, expectations, and knowledge of others all contribute to our interpretation of a person's behavior one way or another.

The personal stories we and others use to make sense of our personal world are called narratives. When we engage in perception checking, we are trying to bridge the gap between different narratives. There are several common perceptual tendencies that lead to inaccurate attributions. Too often we make snap judgments without enough knowledge or information. This leads to stereotyping, in which we seek out isolated behaviors that support our beliefs. We often judge ourselves more charitably than we judge others. This self-serving bias, an egocentric tendency, permits us to have harsh opinions of others for doing the same things we do. Research also shows that people who are aware of the positive and negative traits of another tend to be more influenced by the negative. As a result, we tend to be influenced by what is most obvious. Labeling people according to first impressions is an inevitable part of the perception process. Even if later proven wrong, we still cling to first impressions. At the same time, we commonly imagine that others possess the same attitudes and motives that we do. We tend to assume others who are like us in age, race, religion, interests, hobbies, employment, school, or even appearance, hold similar views, opinions, and likes and dislikes.

One solution to the communication challenge of differing perceptions is empathy. Empathy is defined as the ability to re-create another person's perspective, to experience the world from the other's point of view. Do not confuse empathy with sympathy. Sympathy differs in that, while a sympathetic person feels compassion for the predicament, he or she lacks the degree of identification that empathy entails. Secondly; sympathy denotes acceptance of the reason that has been given for the predicament.

A good way to handle interpretations of perception is to perform perception checking. A complete perception check has three parts: a description of the behavior you have noticed, at least two possible interpretations, and a request for clarification. Because its goal is mutual understanding, perception checking is a cooperative approach to communication.

People use communication strategies to influence how others view them. This is referred to as identity management. The perceived self is a reflection of self-concept. This "face" is the person you believe you are in moments of honest self-examination. In contrast to the perceived self, the presenting self is our public image, the way we want to appear to others. In most cases, this "facework" is what we seek to create in a socially approved image. One characteristic of identity management is the availability of multiple identities. Another characteristic is the collaborative nature of identity-related communication. In most cases, identity management is a conscious effort to deliberately present your self in a certain way. In other cases, we unconsciously act in ways that are really small public performances.

Why bother trying to shape others' opinions? Social rules govern our behavior in a variety of settings. Good manners are often aimed at making others more comfortable. Or we might manage our identity to accomplish personal goals. In certain situations aggressive identity management is not considered deception but, rather, putting your best foot forward to meet social needs and further your acceptance by others.

At first glance, computer-generated communication seems to have limited potential for identity management. There is a lack of obvious physical nonverbal cues and a matter of richness to contend with. But impressions can be made via clarity or ambiguity of language, seriousness or humor, logic or emotion. Asynchronous forms of communication allow you to edit, rewrite, compose, and say difficult things without forcing an immediate response. Both face-to-face and social media forms can be manipulated to create the impression you want people to have.

In countless situations every day, you have a choice about your identity management. There is no single honest way to behave. Impression management involves deciding which part and how much of yourself to reveal. Not all misrepresentations are intentional. There can be a gap between participants' self-perceptions and a more objective assessment. While honesty is an admirable trait, revealing too much too fast and/or being completely truthful rarely are appropriate.

Chapter 3: Key Terms

For each of these items, define the term, give an example, and explain the significance of the term.

1.   empathy

2.   ethnocentrism

3.   facework

4.   face

5.   identity management

6.   interpretation

7.   narrative

8.   organization

9.   perceived self

10.   presenting self
11.   selection

12.   self-concept

13.   self-esteem

14.   self-fulfilling prophecy

15.   self-serving bias

16.   significant other

17.   stereotyping

18.   sympathy

Chapter 3: Review Questions

These questions are designed to help you understand this chapter's concepts and express your understanding in your own words. For practice with true/false and multiple- choice questions, use the course website.

1. Define self-concept and list, in one minute's time, as many characteristics as possible that describe you.

2. What is the connection between the phenomenon of the self-fulfilling prophecy and your success or failure in performing a challenging task?

3. As we sort out and make sense of others' behaviors, we form perceptions. Three steps impact our opinions. Identify the three, and explain clearly the impact of each.

4. Research has uncovered several common perceptual tendencies that, through attribution, often cause inaccurate and troublesome perceptions. What are these errors?

5. A student entering class slips and awkwardly falls to the floor. Explain the difference between having empathy versus sympathy for this student.

6. The ability to construct multiple identities is one element of communication competence. What are the other characteristics of identity management?

7. You and a companion are about to enter a restaurant when a battered, rusty, noisy pickup truck of 1970s vintage comes to rest in a handicapped zone. Two loud, vulgar, grimy, staggering men get out of the truck and push past you on their way in the door. You turn to your friend and say, "Let's go somewhere else. They eat here, then I don't." What just happened?

   _____ you anticipated the self-fulfilling prophecy

   _____ you avoided compromising communication competence

   _____ you adapted your identity to cope with confrontation

   _____ you committed several common perceptual errors

   _____ you decided hunger was not a practical nor social need

8. Given the choice, you select applying for a job via computer-mediated communication rather than face to face. What identity management opportunities have you obtained?

   _____ you can now demonstrate your appreciation of cultural differences

   _____ you have avoided low self-esteem by asserting control

   _____ you have the time to present a face of clarity, seriousness, and logic

   _____ you can assume that the employer is as computer literate as you are

_____ your narrative can be adapted to avoid the risk of being too honest

Chapter 3: Thinking Outside the Box: Synthesizing Your Knowledge

These questions are designed to help you develop the big picture by blending what you've learned in this chapter and elsewhere.

1. The job application asks for your faults and your strengths. How do you match your self-concept to the presenting self others view in such as way as to be honest but not to the point of ruining your chances for employment?

2. When communicators come from different cultures or cocultures, the potential for misunderstandings is strong. Search your memory for the most recent encounter you had in which ethnocentrism may have flavored your perception.

Chapter 3: Answers to Review Questions

Your answers should include the following:

1. *Self- concept is defined as a set of relatively stable perceptions that each of us*
   holds about ourself. It includes what we think is unique and what makes us similar or different from others.   A quick one-minute list of characteristics will most likely include age, gender, ethnicity, physical appearance, values, social traits, religion, talents or skills, intellect, political opinions, likes and dislikes, social or economic standing, friendships, achievements, and occupation. Given more time, this list could be hundreds—even thousands—of words long and still not be a complete and accurate depiction of our self-concept.

2. *A self-fulfilling prophecy occurs when a person's expectation of an outcome, and subsequent behavior, makes the outcome more likely to occur than would otherwise have been true. Your expectations influence your own behavior. If you feel anxious about speaking in public, you often act apprehensive, which is interpreted by others as uncertainty and doubt. Their reaction is one of skepticism, and you read that to be proof that you are not an accomplished speaker. That confirms your original self-concept. At other times, one person's expectations govern another's actions. In other words, treating someone as incompetent and underachieving can reinforce feelings of*

low self-esteem, with the result that the individual continues to exhibit incompetence and underachievement. Both versions shape self-concept and thus behavior of yourself and others.

3. We sort out and make sense of others' behavior in three steps: selection, organization, and interpretation. Stimuli that are intense often attract our attention. Contrast and change gets our attention. Intensity and emotional state help shape what we notice about others. We then arrange the information in some meaningful way by using physicality, interaction, and psychological internal perception. Then we interpret the perceptions depending on our degrees of involvement, relational satisfaction, personal experience, assumptions, expectations, and knowledge of others.

4. Listing in no particular rank of influence: we make snap judgments, we often judge ourselves more charitably than we judge others, we pay more attention to negative impressions than to positive ones, we are influenced by what is most obvious, we cling to first impressions even if later proven wrong, and we tend to assume that others are similar to us.

5. Empathy is the ability to re-create another person's perspective, to experience the world from the other's point of view. Empathy requires an understanding that suspends judgment and allows us to experience the feelings that others have. And with empathy there is a genuine concern for the welfare of the other. Sympathy consists of feeling compassion without a personal sense of what the other's predicament is like. Sympathy lacks the degree of identification that empathy entails. When you sympathize, it is with respect to the other's confusion, pain, embarrassment, or frustration. When you empathize, the experience becomes your own.

6. Along with the ability to construct multiple identities, identity management entails collaboration to provide an arena in which all communicators construct their identities in response to the behaviors of others. Identity management can be a conscious act or spontaneous without preplanning, an unconscious process without advance preparation. People differ in their degree of identity management. Some are acutely aware and monitor their facework consistently. Others express what they think and feel without much attention to the impression their behavior creates.

7. Your statement reflects several common perceptual errors.

8. *Computer-mediated communication can give one the time to present clarity instead of ambiguity, to indicate seriousness as opposed to humor, and appear logical rather than emotional.*

Chapter 3: Answers to Thinking Outside the Box

1. *Answers will vary widely, but everyone has faced the need to choose between circumspect language and bluntness. Managing identities does not necessarily make you a liar, and often discretion and tact are admirable qualities to exhibit. The unethical use of manipulation, lies, deceit, false pretenses, and ulterior motives is strongly discouraged. However, our reflected appraisal must be occasionally reshaped to accommodate restraint and delicacy. If the perceived self runs counter to the presenting self, both identity management and self-concept suffer challenges. An interesting internal debate over how much is "too much" often ensues. Be advised: you may not want to reveal everything; you should realize that complete honesty is often inappropriate.*

2. *While each experience is unique, culture provides a filter that influences the way we interpret correctness and appropriateness. Different cultures and cocultures view similar aspects of behavior, from hand gestures to directness of language, through different perceptual lenses. Eye contact, volume or the lack thereof, posture, attitude, and even blinking are viewed from the standpoint of assumed ethnocentric superiority of traditions, standards, and procedures. Cross-cultural differences can be quite subtle, and yet they may unconsciously cause revamped perceptual tendencies. Awareness of perspective checking improves communication competence; but only when people recognize the differences among standards of behavior can they adapt to one another, or at least understand and respect the differences.*

CHAPTER 4: LANGUAGE

SQ3R in Action:

Generate an SQ3R chart for this chapter here:
http://www.teach-nology.com/web_tools/graphic_org/sq3r

Survey

Skim the title, Chapter Highlights, objectives ("You should understand" and "You should be able to"), headings, tables, photos, cartoons, figures, charts, and items in the margin. Glance at the titles of the Critical Thinking Probes and Ethical Challenges. At the end of each chapter, look over the list of Key Terms, Activities, and Resources.

Question

Ask yourself questions. What do you know about these topics from your own life experiences and from other classes? Ask these six questions in each section: who, what, when, where, how, and why.

Read

Take one heading at a time and read to find the answers to the questions you've posed.

Recite

In your own words, say the answer aloud and then write it out.

Review

Review each section and then review the whole chapter. This is a good time to use the activities at the end of each chapter and the activities and the sample exam on the course website. Remember to periodically review the preceding chapters as well.

Chapter 4: Outline

(Italicized words are key terms.)

   I.   The complexity of *language* is a tool to more skillfully improve everyday interaction.
      A.   Language is defined as a collection of *symbols* governed by rules and used to convey messages between individuals.
      B.   Arbitrary constructions representing thoughts are given meaning by people
      C.   Language contains *phonological, syntactic, semantic,* and pragmatic rules.
  II.   The way we use language influences others and reflects our attitudes.
      A.   Language shapes our ideas of others by means of naming, as well as by showing (or not) credibility, status, sexism, racism, vulgarity, and labeling.
      B.   Language reflects our own attitudes through power, affiliation of *convergence* or *divergence*, attraction and interest, and responsibility.
      C.   Responsibility is accepted or rejected with "it" versus "I" statements, "you" versus "I" statements, "but" statements, or by asking a question rather than making a declaration.
 III.   Most linguistic misunderstandings arise from some common problems easily remedied.
      A.   The use of *equivocal words, relative words, slang, jargon,* and overly *abstract language* causes confusion and misunderstanding.
      B.   Disruptive language such as confusing *factual statements* with *opinion statements,* or confusing facts with *inferential statements*, or using *emotive language* to announce an attitude can be troublesome.
      C.   Some *euphemisms* are pretentious and confusing, while *equivocation* can be interpreted as deliberately ambiguous.
 IV.   There are significant differences between the way men and women speak.
      A.   Content of conversations, reasons for communicating, the style of presentation, and social philosophy affect communication.
      B.   Social orientation, the *sex role* of the communicator, governs behavior;. Masculinity and femininity are culturally recognized, however; they are not biological traits.
  V.   Differences in the way language is used across cultures makes communication a challenging task.
      A.   *Low-context* and *high-context* cultures vary in the use of verbal communication styles.
      B.   Low- and high-context cultures also vary in terms of whether they are see as elaborate or succinct.

C.   A third way languages differ from one culture to another involves formality and informality.

D.   Linguistic relativism is the notion of a worldview of a culture being shaped and reflected by the language its members speak.

Chapter 4: Summary

Language is a complex and often confusing but quite necessary tool for communication. Language is defined as a collection of symbols governed by rules and used to convey messages between individuals. The arbitrary constructions known as symbols represent a communicator's thoughts; but quite often the meanings assigned to those symbols are internal, not general. Words don't mean, people do, and often in widely different ways.

Language contains several types of rules. Phonological rules govern how words sound. Syntactic rules govern the structure of language. Semantic rules deal with the meaning of specific words. Pragmatic rules govern how people use language in everyday interaction. There are several levels at which the rules each person uses differ because of self-concept, the episode being discussed, perceived relationships, and cultural backgrounds.

How language is used can shape ideas, values, beliefs, and attitudes. Names affect the way we regard a person or object. Credibility is a strong influence on perception, as are indicators of status. This is often conveyed through language. Attitudes are often shaped beyond individual cases and applied to entire groups of people because of sexism and racism in language. Labeling and stereotyping causes the out-group to be set apart and pictured in an unfavorable light. The use of vulgar and offensive language influences our interaction with others.

When we use language with power, it reflects back on us by indicating control; whereas powerless language signifies less influence. Language can be used to build solidarity by showing a commonality, an affiliation, between communicators. This convergence contrasts with the strategy of divergence, or setting one self apart from others. Linguistic intergroup bias reflects whether we do or do not regard others as part of our in-group. Language can suggest a degree of interest or attraction toward a person, object, or idea. Indications of a willingness to accept responsibility, or not, are conveyed through language. Saying "you" instead of "I" in statements, and blaming "tt" rather that "I," are ways of shifting responsibility for the content away from the speaker. Including "but" in a statement cancels everything that went before, and phrasing a message in the form of a question rather than making a declaration indicates that the speaker declines to accept responsibility.

Most linguistic misunderstandings arise from some common problems that are easily remedied. Avoid equivocal words that have more than one dictionary meaning. Being precise is preferred to using relative words of comparison. For example, how long is "soon"? Language specialized to a group of people whose members belong to a similar coculture is called slang. Jargon is vocabulary that functions as a sort of shorthand for people with common backgrounds or experiences. Both can be confusing. Abstract language refers only vaguely to events or objects and can result in stereotyping and behavioral descriptions that cause conflict.

Disruptive language causes confusion when factual statements are forsaken for opinion statements. Sometimes factual statements are replaced by inferential statements. One way to avoid this confusion is to use the perception-checking skill described in Chapter 2. When communicators use words describing but at the same time announcing their attitude, the emotive language may sound like a statement of fact; in reality, though, it is an expression of feelings. Language that reflects emotion can cause disruptive communication. More frustrating and confusing to some is the appearance of being misleading, antagonistic, or reluctant to express an opinion. Euphemisms have been in our lexicon since birth, but substituting a pleasant term in place of a direct, potentially more offensive one can be unsettling. As with euphemisms, most equivocation is seen as an act of substitution. This is often interpreted as vague and ambiguous. Despite the advantage of avoiding uncomfortable or embarrassing situations, whether to use equivocation is often an ethical decision for the would-be competent communicator.

Do men and women employ different communication styles? There are similarities, but there are also differences. One difference is in the content of the communication. As a generalization, females spend more time discussing personal and domestic subjects, whereas men discuss current events, sports, and business. Men and women equally discuss personal appearance and sex; however women tend to gossip most about close friends and family, whereas men gossip over sports figures and celebrities. One researcher states that women use talk as the essence of relationships. Men are more likely to use language to accomplish the job at hand. Women ask more questions in mixed-sex conversations. Men interrupt more. Women are more accommodating to the topics men raise, and topics introduced by men are more likely to be pursued. Social philosophy and occupation influence speaking styles, but most powerful is the communicator's sex role. This social orientation, rather than biological gender, is what governs communication behavior. As situations and circumstances become more equal over time, the differences between male and female use of language will become smaller.

Each language, and the interpretation of that language, has its own unique style that poses a challenge when one is communicating across cultures. Low-context and high-context cultures value directness of language differently. The stylistic clash between cultures or cocultures arises because some value elaborate, rich expressive language and others prefer succinctness to the point of silence. Formal tone and delivery are of great concern to some, whereas others prefer a casual, informal delivery. Different linguistic styles separate speakers of various cultures often, given that linguistic relativism starts early in life. The notion that the worldview of a culture is shaped and reflected by the language its members speak has been put forth by some to explain the ethnocentric pride each culture places in its language.

Chapter 4: Key Terms

For each of these terms, define the term, give an example, and explain the significance of the term.

1. abstract language

2. abstraction ladder

3. convergence

4. divergence

5. language

6. linguistic intergroup bias

7. descriptive communication

8. emotive language

9. equality

10. equivocal language

11. equivocal words

12. equivocation

13. euphemism

14. factual statement

15.   high-context culture

16.   inferential statement

17.   jargon

18.   language

19.   linguistic determinism

20.   linguistic relativism

21.   low-context culture

22.   opinion statement

23.   phonological rules

24.   relative words

25.   Sapir–Whorf hypothesis

26.   semantic rules

27.   sex role

28.   slang

29.   symbols

30.   syntactic rules

Chapter 4: Review Questions

These questions are designed to help you understand this chapter's concepts and express your understanding in your own words. For practice with true/false and multiple- choice questions, use the course website.

1.   Define language and create four examples demonstrating the application of each rule that governs language.

2.   Language shapes attitudes through at least four various methods. Use your experiences to cite a "for instance" of each from recent conversations.

3. Competent communicators realize that the use of language reflects on them and their attitudes. This interpretation comes about because of what contributing factors?

4. Create four compare-and-contrast examples of the ways language is used to accept or reject responsibility.

5. Most semantic misunderstandings arise from some common problems that are easily remedied. Identify the troublesome language you might encounter on a typical school day.

6. Briefly explain the key differences between how men and women use language.

7. Sugar looks longingly in the jewelry store window and says to her boyfriend, "It's calling my name. You realize I love you but why don't you have enough money?" This is an example of what?

    _____ using euphemisms to avoid being too direct and confrontational

    _____ cocultural difficulty with the ethnocentric needs of women

    _____ improper use of accepted language rules depicting symbolism

    _____ language reflecting the credibility and status of the communicator

    _____ language used to reject responsibility

8. Juan, Shaniqua, Boris, and Nok are assigned to work together on a presentation. Bubba mutters loudly, "Good luck with them getting along." This sarcastic observation proves what?

    _____ the meaning depends upon the person not the word

    _____ names can cause labeling and stereotyping

    _____ equivocation should not be used in a classroom

    _____ slang dominates the age-related coculture of this group

    _____ credibility will be a challenge for anything else said by Bubba

Chapter 4: Thinking Outside the Box: Synthesizing Your Knowledge

These questions are designed to help you develop the big picture by blending what you've learned in this chapter and elsewhere.

1. Consider the notion of linguistic relativism and relate your most recent interpretation challenges in communicating across cultures or cocultures.

2. In theory, we value people who "tell it like it is" and consider "beating around the bush" to be a sign of weakness; in practice, however, we often react differently. Why?

Chapter 4: Answers to Review Questions

Your answers should include the following.

1. *Language is defined as a collection of symbols governed by rules and used to convey messages between individuals. Those rules include phonological rules governing how words sound. For example: A farm can produce fresh produce. Syntactic rules govern the structure of language. For example: "You joke tell? Is to laugh?" violates rules of Englishsyntax. Semantic rules deal with the meaning of specific words. "Down" can mean a direction or the soft undercoat of a duck. Communicators have to agree on the interpretation. Pragmatic rules govern how people use language in everyday applications; thus we all know what is meant by saying, "Please turn the light on."*

2. *You have had personal experiences of being teased about your name, of judging someone's credibility based on how the person uses language, and on assuming or doubting the credibility of someone from the language the individual uses. Language is the usual indicator that someone is feigning status by "putting on airs" and "acting better than me." Upon witnessing sexist and racist language from a stranger, your first inclination is to acknowledge that the person has not made a favorable impression. Offensive and vulgar language can be intrusive and troublesome.*

3. *We reflect attitudes back on our self through the use of power and control in language. Communicators indicate solidarity and affiliation in a variety of ways but most certainly from choice of vocabulary, rate of speech, and even through the level of politeness. This convergence is a linguistic accommodation, but not everyone participates in it. Sometimes the communicator wants to be set apart from others and*

uses divergence to signal difference. Sentences, phrases, and expressions can reflect the communicator's attraction and interest, likes and dislikes. Language can also reveal the speaker's willingness or reluctance to accept responsibility.

4.   *Statements using "it" versus "I," "you" versus" "I," adding "but" after a few positive words, or asking a question rather than making a declaration all indicate unwillingness to accept responsibility: "It won't open" rather than "I cannot open this door." "You always run late" compared to "I am in a hurry." "I like you but . . ." usually means that the next thing said will be uncomplimentary, and " Are you going out dressed like that?" conveys a doubling up of responsibility rejection.*

5.   *Equivocal words and expressions surround us daily. "Get out of here" does not mean to actually leave. "How are you doing?" is not an inquiry regarding your health, and "What's up?" should not generate the response "The opposite of down." We use relative words as comparisons, hoping the other understands. The nearest fast-food place is "not far"; but if you had to walk to it during a downpour, it would then become " too far." "Old" is a description you use to refer to your professor; but a third grader would say that of you. The meaning of a simple term often is relative. You no longer announce to everyone that you are going to go "number one." That euphemistic children's phrase is awkward and uncomfortable. No one is fat today. Instead, people are healthy, big-boned, robust, well-fed, or plus size. These words are less offensive. Your textbook has an ISBN. This is bookstore jargon. Words and phrases considered exclusive to a similar coculture are slang and sound natural in your environment but would be incongruous if said by your grandparent.*

6.   *Generally speaking, the content of the communication varies. Women are more personal and relationship oriented, whereas men seek to achieve goals. Women tend to suggest more passively; men offer advice with more force. Women exhibit a tendency to ask questions in mixed-sex conversations, and men often interrupt. Masculine, feminine, and androgynous sex roles are not designated by biology but rather by behavior.*

7.   *The use of "it," "you," "but," and a question rather than a declaration all indicate that Sugar is rejecting responsibility.*

8.   *Bubba's observation proves that names can cause labeling and stereotyping.*

Chapter 4: Answers to Thinking Outside the Box

1. *Although your answer will vary from those of others as a result of personal experiences, the general concept of coping with the notion that the worldview of your culture is shaped and reflected by the language you and your members speak strengthens your opinion that they, the out-group, should adjust their language to you, a member of the in-group. Translations involve more than words. Actions, tones, directness, richness, context, elaboration or succinctness, formality or informality present interpretation challenges. Cultural identity affects the consciousness and communication competence of everyone involved in the effort; and language, most often, is the first obstacle that must be overcome.*

2. *There is a fine line of distinction between being honest and being blunt. Politeness is often preferred over rudeness. The truth can sometimes hurt, as in commenting too frankly on someone's new hairdo or a child's first effort at sculpting. When a vague or ambiguous response prevents embarrassment or pain, you will sometimes prefer to use it. Deceit, lies, avoidance, and noncommitment are looked on with disdain, but "sugarcoating" can soften the pain. Too much honesty can be inappropriate.*

CHAPTER 5: LISTENING

SQ3R in Action:

Generate an SQ3R chart for this chapter here:
http://www.teach-nology.com/web_tools/graphic_org/sq3r

Survey

Skim the title, Chapter Highlights, objectives ("You should understand" and "You should be able to"), headings, tables, photos, cartoons, figures, charts, and items in the margin. Glance at the titles of the Critical Thinking Probes and Ethical Challenges. At the end of each chapter, look over the list of Key Terms, Activities, and Resources.

Question

Ask yourself questions. What do you know about these topics from your own life experiences and from other classes? Ask these six questions in each section: who, what, when, where, how, and why.

Read

Take one heading at a time and read to find the answers to the questions you've posed.

Recite

In your own words, say the answer aloud and then write it out.

Review

Review each section and then review the whole chapter. This is a good time to use the activities at the end of each chapter and the activities and the sample exam on the course website. Remember to periodically review the preceding chapters as well.

Chapter 5: Outline

(Italicized words are key terms.)

I. We spend more time in *listening* to others than in any other type of communication.
    A. Listening and *hearing* are not the same thing because listening requires *attending*, *understanding*, *responding*, and *remembering*.
    B. Listening is not a natural process, nor do all speakers receive the same message from the same spoken communication.
    C. Listening requires effort to separate *mindless listening* from *mindful listening*.
II. Too often we employ faulty listening behaviors that prevent understanding.
    A. *Pseudolistening* imitates paying attention but is not the real thing.
    B. *Selective listeners* respond only to parts that interest them, and *defensive listeners* are distrustful and suspicious.
    C. *Ambushers* set traps to attack, and *insulated listeners* avoid selected topics.
    D. *Insensitive listeners* take remarks at face value, and *stage hogs* are conversational narcissists.
III. There are several reasons for poor listening.
    A. Message overload, rapid thought, and all three types of noise make for poor listening.
    B. Faulty assumptions, talking instead of listening, and cultural and media influences hinder effective listening.
    C. Not every one listens the same way. There are *content-oriented*, *people-oriented*, *action-oriented*, and *time-oriented listeners*.
IV. When you want to understand another person, you use *informational listening*.
    A. The steps of informational listening include not arguing or prejudging prematurely, separating the message from the speaker, and searching for value.
    B. Other components of informational listening are looking for key ideas, asking *sincere questions* not *counterfeit questions*, *paraphrasing*, and taking notes.
V. When you listen to judge the quality of the message with a view to accepting or rejecting it, you employ *critical listening*.
    A. Reserve judging credibility until you are certain you understand the message.
    B. Look for credible support by examining the speaker's evidence and reasoning. Examine the emotional appeals that may influence your ability to apply logic.
VI. The goal of one very important communication skill, *supportive listening*, is to build a relationship or help solve a problem.

A.   The types of supportive response commonly used include *advising response*, *judging response*, *analyzing statements*, *questioning*, *comforting,* and *prompting*.

B.   Other supportive listeners might use *reflecting* combined with paraphrasing; but before choosing that type of response, they should always consider the situation, the other person, and personal strengths and weaknesses.

Chapter 5: Summary

Listening easily qualifies as the most important kind of communication. In spite of its importance, the activity itself is misunderstood because some assume listening and hearing are the same. That is not the case. Listening differs because it involves attending, understanding, responding, and remembering. It is not a natural process. Everybody does it, though few people do it well. Listening is a skill. Not all listeners receive the same message. Given the wide range of possible perceptions and individual thought processes, it is unrealistic to expect to find uniform comprehension.

Mindful listening requires effort. Given the number of incoming messages our brains absorb, the belief that we listen carefully, diligently, and with 100% attention at all times is implausible. Mindless listening is not a negative connotation. It is reality. When careful listening is taking place, the effort is similar to physical activity in that the heart rate quickens, respiration increases, and body temperature rises.

There are several faulty listening behaviors we engage in that prevent effective listening. Pseudolistening is an imitation of the real thing. There can be eye contact and head nodding, but the brain is otherwise occupied. Selective listeners respond only to parts of a speaker's remarks that interest them; it is a process of picking and choosing. Defensive listeners pay close attention because they interpret innocent comments as personal attacks. They are distrustful, suspicious, and insecure. Ambush listening means that one listens with care but with the intent of lying in wait to rebut a point or spring a trap. Insulated listeners avoid topics. They block out or turn off messages that contain unwanted content. Insensitive listeners do not look behind the words or behavior for meaning but rather take things at face value. They get their feelings hurt a lot. Then there are the more egotistic listeners, refocusing all messages to aim the spotlight on themselves. These stage hogs are conversational narcissists.

Still, there are times when circumstances, situations, and personal interests cause poor listening. Oftentimes the listener suffers a message overload. When the brain is bombarded with too much information, too rapidly, the listener shuts down and receives little or nothing. And yet, spoken information can be delivered too slowly. Boredom and the need for stimulation cause poor listening because the brain works faster than the average person talks. Our rapid thought outpaces most input. Noise often causes poor listening. Internal psychological noise, external physical noise, and physiological hearing problems often frustrate and hinder effective listening. We often do not listen because we do not value the input. Faulty assumptions and preconceived ideas lead to dismissing the comments without actually listening to them. We are all aware that it is easier to talk than to listen. Talking has more apparent advantages. Talking casually does not require the thought process or the effort of listening. Earlier chapters referred to cultural challenges in communication, and that includes listening. How one speaks and how one listens can be a product of culture. Lastly, the contemporary social and mass media of today's society discourages focused attention and concentration. Brevity and headlines often are substituted for clarity and depth. Details are bothersome—immediacy rules.

Not everyone listens the same way. Content-oriented listeners want details and specifics. People-oriented listeners are concerned about feelings and relationships with others. Action-oriented listeners focus on the task at hand, since accomplishment and achievement are their goals. Time-oriented listeners are most concerned with efficiency.

When you actively listen to understand another person, you are exercising the approach known as informational listening. To do this effectively, you must realize that you should not prejudge, and you cannot argue until you have received the message; then you must separate the message from the speaker. Listening with a constructive attitude is important. You should focus on the key idea or central point, using your natural ability to think faster than the speaker talks. Asking questions is beneficial, as long as the questions are sincere and not counterfeit. Paraphrasing is a useful tool to aid understanding. Restating in your own words the message you think the speaker has sent enhances clarity. Comprehension is reinforced if you take notes. Measures that make it possible to complement your memory come in both physical and mental forms.

You will not agree with everything. Some input should be examined and evaluated. A critical listener judges the quality of a message in order to decide whether to accept of reject it. One necessary step in becoming an efficient critical listener is to listen before evaluating. You must get the message and then judge it. Evaluate the speaker's credibility. Acceptability of an idea often depends on its source. Be insistent on receiving evidence and reasoning. What support solidifies the contention? Demand verification. Too often a listener allows emotion to overrule logic. Examine the emotional appeals.

Social support has been shown to be among the most important communication skills. Supportive listening is used to build a relationship or help solve a problem. As a group, women are more likely than men to give emotional support to another's personal problem. Men offer advice and then change the subject, often challenging the individual to evaluate his or her attitudes and values. Competent supportive listeners offer a solution via an advising response. Sometimes they will evaluate the sender's thoughts or behaviors and issue a judging response. Interpretation is useful in supportive listening. An analyzing statement can be used to consider alternative meanings. Stimulating thinking is a useful element undertaken by questioning. Questions trigger examination. Sometimes one is asked to listen to provide support in the way of comfort or prompting. Encouragement takes several forms: agreement, praise, reassurance, diversion, or acknowledgment. A listener can be a catalyst who helps others find their own answers. Moments of reflection are used not so much to clarify the listener's goals as to help the speaker absorb and consider the very words spoken.

Before committing to the obligation of listening, you can boost your odds of choosing the best helping style by considering the situation, the other person, and your own strengths and weaknesses. Listening is work and a work-in-progress. Be aware and listen with care.

Chapter 5: Key Terms

For each of these terms, define the term, give an example, and explain the significance of the term.

1. action-oriented listening

2. advising response

3. ambushing

4. analyzing statement

5. attending

6. comforting

7. content-oriented listening

8. counterfeit question

9. critical listening

10. defensive listening

11. hearing

12. informational listening

13. insensitive listening

14.   insulated listening

15.   judging response

16.   listening

17.   listening fidelity

18.   mindful listening

19.   mindless listening

20.   paraphrasing

21.   people-oriented listening

22.   prompting

23.   pseudolistening

24.   questioning

25.   reflecting

26.   remembering

27.   residual message

28.   responding

29.   selective listening

30.   sincere question

31.   stage hogging

32.   supportive listening

33.   time-oriented listening

34.   understanding

Chapter 5: Review Questions

These questions are designed to help you understand this chapter's concepts and express your understanding in your own words. For practice with true/false and multiple- choice questions, use the course website.

1. What are the fundamental differences between listening and hearing? Explain mindful listening in comparison to mindless listening.

2. Categorize the most obvious faulty listening behaviors.

3. There are reasons—some acceptable, some not—for poor listening. What are they?

4. Not everyone listens the same way. Identify the different listening orientations, and give an example of each.

5. Define informational listening and detail the necessary components involved.

6. Being skeptical and cynical is useful with critical listening. Define this skill, and cite the procedures used by successful critical listeners.

7. Empathy is vital when you are listening supportively. What is the definition of supportive listening? What stylistic inputs are essential?

8. Chris is watching a football game. His wife tells him that she has to go out of town on business the next weekend. Chris looks at her, nods, and goes back to the game. Later he is surprised to see her packing. Why?

   _____ his wife was not in the same coculture as Chris

   _____ Chris was guilty of pseudolistening

   _____ Chris failed to paraphrase a response

   _____ his wife is people oriented and Chris is time oriented

   _____ Chris applied critical listening unfairly

9. Alicia listens intently to the student debate in class but often finds herself voting for the classmates she likes the best. Alicia is most likely guilty of what?

   _____ action-oriented listening

   _____ critical listening

_____ incomprehensible response

_____ informational listening

_____ people-oriented listening

Chapter 5: Thinking Outside the Box: Synthesizing Your Knowledge

These questions are designed to help you develop the big picture by blending what you've learned in this chapter and elsewhere.

1. Pick a recent communication experience in which your listening has been somehow inadequate. It can be from school, your place of worship, or work, or from social exchanges. Use what you now know about faulty listening behaviors and reasons for poor listening to explain in detail why you did not fully "get" the message.

2. Have you ever sought supportive listening via mediated social communication? If yes, why? If no, why not? Justify your answer.

Chapter 5: Answers to Review Questions

Your answers should include the following:

1. *Listening differs from hearing because it involves attending, understanding, responding, and remembering. Applying the effort to match the degree of congruence between what a listener understands and what the message sender was attempting to communicate requires concentration. Responsiveness, either verbal or nonverbal, indicates participation in the process. Retention requires involvement. A passive listener is a mindless listener—neither focusing nor exercising the care necessary for effective listening.*

2. *Pseudolistening, selective listening, defensive listening, ambush listening, insulated listening, insensitive listening, and stage hogging.*

3. *Message overload, rapid thought, psychological noise, physical noise, hearing problems, faulty assumptions, talking has more advantages, cultural differences, and media influences.*

4.   *Content-oriented listeners seek details. Not only do they want to know why the car would not start, they want an analysis of the complexity of the engine. People-oriented listeners respond to feelings and relationships. Suppose the mechanic says the car will not be repaired until next week. The people-oriented listener may conclude that the mechanic is overworked, underpaid, and needs more time with the family. Action-oriented listeners want results. Fix the car now! Time-oriented listeners are most concerned with efficiency. They would want a set date and a precise deadline for the repairs to be completed.*

5.   *Informational listening is the approach taken when you want to understand what another person has said. To ensure that you receive the same thoughts as the speaker, you cannot argue or begin your evaluation prematurely. You have to separate the message from the speaker, search for value, look for key ideas, ask questions, paraphrase, and take notes.*

6.   *To be a critical listener, you must judge the quality of a message in order to decide whether to accept or reject it. To do that effectively, you must listen for information before evaluating, gauge the speaker's credibility, examine the speaker's evidence and reasoning, and review any emotional appeals that have been used.*

7.   *The goal of supportive listening is to build a relationship or help the speaker solve a problem. Approaches to supportive listening include advising responses, judging responses, an analyzing statement, questioning, comforting, prompting, reflecting, and paraphrasing.*

8.   *Chris was guilty of pseudolistening.*

9.   *Alicia's actions fit the definition of a people-oriented listener.*

Chapter 5: Answers to Thinking Outside the Box

1.   *The situation, the other person involved, and your self-reflection should provide ample ammunition for appraisal of the listening experience you chose. Recognizing faulty listening behaviors is the first step toward improving your communication skills. Listening skills are crucial in education, work, daily applications, and personal relationships. Overcoming the many reasons for poor listening is a challenge, but an effective listener realizes the impossibility of communicating unless someone receives the message.*

2. *With the growth of the social media community has come an expansion of personal information being shared with strangers or casual acquaintances. Often the communicators have not met face to face and may not know the other people's names. Identity management is much easier when there are few nonverbal messages being detected and sifted for clues. The social media offer an anonymity that can overcome shyness and prop up the courage of people who otherwise would hesitate to reveal medical conditions, eating disorders, political opinions, religious affiliation, addictions, and sexual proclivity. In fact, social media communicators typically open up faster and with more depth than do partners in a traditional face-to-face exchange. Delayed response and time to edit is a comfort to some, in a way relaxing them and making them more receptive to the challenge of being effective listeners. Some are comfortable with this channel, some are not. Culture, age, and past experiences are major contributors to social media relationships.*

CHAPTER 6: NONVERBAL COMMUNICATION

SQ3R in Action:

Generate an SQ3R chart for this chapter here:
http://www.teach-nology.com/web_tools/graphic_org/sq3r

Survey

Skim the title, Chapter Highlights, objectives ("You should understand" and "You should be able to"), headings, tables, photos, cartoons, figures, charts, and items in the margin. Glance at the titles of the Critical Thinking Probes and Ethical Challenges. At the end of each chapter, look over the list of Key Terms, Activities, and Resources.

Question

Ask yourself questions. What do you know about these topics from your own life experiences and from other classes? Ask these six questions in each section: who, what, when, where, how, and why.

Read

Take one heading at a time and read to find the answers to the questions you've posed.

Recite

In your own words, say the answer aloud and then write it out.

Review

Review each section and then review the whole chapter. This is a good time to use the activities at the end of each chapter and the activities and the sample exam on the course website. Remember to periodically review the preceding chapters as well.

Chapter 6: Outline

(Italicized words are key terms.)

I. It is virtually impossible to avoid using *nonverbal communication*.
   A. The definition of *nonverbal* covers messages expressed through nonlinguistic means.
   B. There is communicative value in nonverbal behavior, but it is primarily relational in interpretation measures.
   C. Because nonverbal behavior is often difficult to interpret, it is ambiguous; sometimes it is presented without conscious effort, and at other times the communicator has not intended to send the message that has been received.
II. There are influences affecting the ability to understand and use nonverbal communication.
   A. Cultural differences and gender differences do exist
   B. Control and the power of insight influence accuracy of interpretation.
III. Several functions of nonverbal communication relate to the verbal forms.
   A. Actions such as repeating, substituting, complementing, and accenting highlight verbal messages
   B. Regulating, contradicting, and deceiving functions of nonverbal communication result from *microexpressions*.
IV. Our bodies, artifacts, environments, and the way we use time all send nonverbal messages.
   A. *Kinesics* and the ability to interpret ambiguous *manipulators* are tools used to send messages.
   B. The face, the eyes, and the *affect blends* presented combine to show messages.
   C. *Paralanguage* originating from the voice, with its *disfluency* and accent, is a nonverbal vehicle.
   D. Appearance and clothing are perception agents used strongly in nonverbal communication.
   E. Touch communicates; and the study of space, *proxemics*, has context relating to *intimate distance*, *personal distance*, *social distance*, and *public distance*.
   F. The environment and the use and structure of time, *chronemics*, can and often do send nonverbal messages.

Chapter 6: Summary

There is often a big gap between what people say and what they feel. Communicators struggle to determine the meaning behind the content. Sending messages expressed through nonlinguistic means is called nonverbal communication. It is virtually impossible to avoid communicating nonverbally. Of course, we do not always intend to convey the meanings received in the nonverbal messages we send. The meaning sometimes depends on the person, not the word. Nonverbal communication is primarily relational but often ambiguous. Our culture, gender, past experiences, assumptions, and listening skills help us in deciphering nonverbal indicators.

Although verbal and nonverbal messages differ in many ways, the two forms operate together most of the time. Nonverbal communication functions in conjunction with the verbal form via repetition. People remember comments accompanied by gestures more than those made with words alone. Substitution delivers nonverbal messages with emblems, deliberate precise meanings known to everyone in a cultural group. In most cultures familiar to westerners, for example, moving the head up and down signals yes. Sometimes behavior and content are in unison, and the function of nonverbal is complementing. That is, the nonverbal part goes along with what is being said to clarify and support the spoken word. Illustrators explain and accompany messages to help convey emotion. Emphasizing a point, a word, or an action underlines and highlights the verbal message through accenting.

At other times, nonverbal behaviors regulate the flow of communication. Starting and stopping are indicated nonverbally. There are degrees of sarcasm we encounter that send mixed messages serving to contradict the associated verbal messages alone. In such cases, when a competent receiver perceives an inconsistency between verbal and nonverbal messages, the nonverbal one carries more weight. Trust plays a big role in communication, and a trusting listener is the recipient of communicative efforts to deceive. Microexpressions such as fleeting facial expressions, subtle changes in enunciation, altered eye contact, and different body language shifts lasting a fraction of a second are "tells" of deception. Usually observers spot deception more easily than designated listeners.

The variety of types of nonverbal communication delivery begins with what is most notable. Body movement stimulates the eye, and the brain offers interpretation. Posture and gesture illustrate and convey messages. Kinesics is the study of body movement, gesture, and posture. Most people cannot express themselves without gesturing. In fact, not gesturing often communicates information, regardless of whether this is intentional. The face and the eyes are most noticeable in face-to-face communication, and their impact is powerful. The prevalence of affect blends, the combining of two or more expressions showing different emotions, contributes to the ambiguity of communication. In and between members of the same culture, the intended interpretation is easier to recognize. Paralanguage, which is sent via nonverbal vocal means, gives voice to messages sent via means other than linguistic. Tone, speed, pitch, volume, number and length of pauses, and disfluencies such as stammering and the insertion of vocal fillers reinforce or contradict the message our words convey. An earlier chapter dealt with the influence of perception in communication, explaining that nonverbal signals come across strongly in the appearance of the communicator. The clues available include physical attractiveness, clothing, hygiene, and identity management.

Physical touch can "speak" volumes. The study of touch in human behavior is called haptics. One reason actions speak louder than words is that touch was the first language device we acquired, in infancy. Touch is personal, intimate, and emotional. The timing and appropriateness of touching elicits strong reactions in the receiver. So too does the use of space. The distance we put between ourselves and others and the territory we consider to be our own sends messages. The study of the way people and animals use space has been termed proxemics. Intimate distance begins with skin contact and ranges out to personal distance, that space or comfort within or outside another's reach. Social distance of conversational situations varies from the comfortable to formal and impersonal to the public distance, which is the point at which two-way communication is challenged. A range so broad suggests that more than one listener is possible and that the communicators are not always intent on a personal dialogue. Whereas personal space is the bubble we carry around as an extension of our physical being, territory is fixed space. A room, a house, a neighborhood, even a country, a library, or a beach can be our territory for ourselves and others we allow in. Generally, we grant those with higher status more personal territory and greater respect for space. The physical environment people create can both reflect and shape interaction. We perceive many impressions from our surroundings. Intelligence, politeness, maturity, optimism, family orientations, artistic interests, desire for privacy, and energy, along with other personality traits, are communicated by the spatial or territorial environment we construct.

The term *chronemics* designates the study of how human beings use and structure time. The use of time as a communication tool depends greatly on the culture. North Americans tend to use time as a signal of status. Showing up late for a job interview is unacceptable. Monochronic societies emphasize punctuality. Polychronic cultures allow flexible schedules and casual approaches to deadlines. In the United States time is used to indicate status and respect. Prestigious people are granted leniency in arriving for scheduled appointments. The time of important people is valuable. Subordinates wait. How quickly you answer a question, or the time it takes you to respond, will send a message as clear as a spoken word.

Chapter 6: Key Terms

For each of these terms, define the term, give an example, and explain the significance of the term.

1.   affect blend

2.   chronemics

3.   disfluency

4.   emblems

5.   illustrators

6.   microexpressions

7.   intimate distance

8.   kinesics

9.   manipulators

10. monochromic

11. nonverbal communication

12. paralanguage

13. personal distance

14. polychromic

15. proxemics

16. public distance

17. social distance

18. territory

Chapter 6: Review Questions

These questions are designed to help you understand this chapter's concepts and express your understanding in your own words. For practice with true/false and multiple- choice questions, use the course website.

1. Define nonverbal communication and its value in facilitating the comprehension of messages.

2. Identify the functions of nonverbal communication. Cite an example for each function listed.

3. Use an example of a situation in which you have interpreted microexpressions to arrive at a measure of trust.

4. Starting with the most notable and completing with the more subtle, list the types of nonverbal communication.

5. You ask your mother to pass the salt and she stares at you without blinking. You turn to your sister and she blows a loud expression of disgust through her lips. Your final appeal is to your dad, who pushes back from the table and leaves. "Okay," you say, "I get it. Never put the turkey in the clothes dryer to thaw." What concept of communication was exhibited by your family?

_____ cultural disfluencies separating the genders

_____ microexpressive proxemics

_____ personal distance, social distance, public distance
_____ paralanguage with haptic illustrators

_____ nonverbal tools of eye contact, facial expressions, voice, and distance

6. Jamie was awakened by her roommate at 5:30 a.m. although she did not have to wake up until 8:00 a.m. Jamie blurted out, "Thanks for waking me up!"
What nonverbal tool was Jamie using?

_____ euphemisms

_____ paralanguage

_____chronemics

_____ relational ambiguity

_____ proxemics

Chapter 6: Thinking Outside the Box: Synthesizing Your Knowledge

These questions are designed to help you develop the big picture by blending what you've learned in this chapter and elsewhere.

1. Phoenix is glaring at Misty. Misty slowly nods her head. Phoenix is standing rigid without making gestures. Misty waits at least 20 seconds and then moves closer. She slowly reaches out and touches Phoenix. Phoenix expels a long slow deep breath and sits down. In your own words, describe your observations and narrate the circumstances, from beginning to end, of the story of Phoenix and Misty.

2. Most people become more successful liars as they grow older. Why?

Chapter 6: Answers to Review Questions

Your answers should include the following:

1. *Nonverbal communication is defined as messages expressed through nonlinguistic means. It has communicative value in revealing information, signaling emotion, accompanying verbal messages, and relating to the other communicators. It plays a role in identity management and perception and, although ambiguous, is expressive and iss an important component of our emotional intelligence.*

2. *The functions of nonverbal communication and an example of each might include beginning by saying the word "first" and at the same time holding up one finger. Using emblems such as head nodding to substitute for verbally saying "yes" typifies another nonverbal act of communication. Holding the hands apart indicating how big the fish was while saying how big it was is an example of complementing. Pointing an accusatory finger while stressing "You!" with the voice adds accent. Lifting a hand in the air before speaking and using inflection of the voice to request cessation of speaking both are examples of regulation via nonverbal functions. A sarcastic remark is a good example of the function of contradicting. And guarding against "giving it away" when someone asks if you know anything about a surprise birthday party typifies the use of nonverbal functions for deception.*

3. *Although this answer has many possible explanations, yours should include the nonverbal behaviors called microexpressions. Did you*

figure out that the belt you'd worn really did not match your outfit despite the verbal messages someone sent? Was it because of your familiarity with the other communicator or because of your intuition and suspicion? Have you ever detected deception in a card game, or in a small-group setting? Unfortunately, experience is the best teacher.

4.   *The types of nonverbal communication include movement, posture and gesture, face and eyes, voice, appearance, attractiveness, clothing, touch, space, territory, the environment, and time.*

5.   *The communication concept exhibited by your family involves the nonverbal tools of eye contact, facial expressions, voice, and distance.*

6.   *Jamie's nonverbal tool of choice is paralanguage.*

Chapter 6: Answers to Thinking Outside the Box

1.   *There is an obvious communication conflict taking place between Phoenix and Misty. Although your interpretation will differ from a classmate's, the nonverbal functions and signs tell an interesting story. At the beginning Phoenix is upset, stubborn, and expecting resistance. Misty is being patient but persistent. With eye contact and substitution as communication devices, both have expressed their emotions. Misty uses time and then changes personal distance into intimate distance and adds touch. Several messages are communicated. Phoenix capitulates reluctantly via vocal expressions and an alteration in body movement and posture. Argument stated, points communicated, decision and resolution accepted. The end.*

2.   *As we get older and acquire more experience, we become adept at controlling and hiding signs of deceit. It is easiest to catch liars when they have not had a chance to rehearse, when they feel strongly about the information being hidden, or when they feel anxious or guilty about their lies. We learn to detect lies by trial and error. Taking advantage of trust increases the possibility of successful deception. An out-of-place smirk or twitch at the edge of the lips, a glance away when intent focus was called for, or too much direct eye contact, a throbbing vein visible where one was not present seconds earlier—these could be indicators of deception. Confidence and practice can eliminate these signs. Fidgeting fingers and restless gestures, changes in vocal rate, tone, and pitch, unnecessary body movement or a movement increasing*

distance, a shift in physical positioning, excessive blinking, and pauses or vocal fillers could be signs of deception. Self-control and firm identity management often hinder would-be detection. Still, you must remember, there are no surefire nonverbal cues that indicate deception. Intimacy can serve as a cloak masking deceptive messages. Once you begin to suspect that a speaker may be lying, you tend to pay closer attention to the nonverbal behavior. Generally, women detect deception more consistently and accurately than men; but women are more inclined to "fall for" the deceptive ploys of intimate partners than are men.

CHAPTER 7:
UNDERSTANDING INTERPERSONAL RELATIONSHIPS

SQ3R in Action:

Generate an SQ3R chart for this chapter here:
http://www.teach-nology.com/web_tools/graphic_org/sq3r

Survey

Skim the title, Chapter Highlights, objectives ("You should understand" and "You should be able to"), headings, tables, photos, cartoons, figures, charts, and items in the margin. Glance at the titles of the Critical Thinking Probes and Ethical Challenges. At the end of each chapter, look over the list of Key Terms, Activities, and Resources.

Question

Ask yourself questions. What do you know about these topics from your own life experiences and from other classes? Ask these six questions in each section: who, what, when, where, how, and why.

Read

Take one heading at a time and read to find the answers to the questions you've posed.

Recite

In your own words, say the answer aloud and then write it out.

Review

Review each section and then review the whole chapter. This is a good time to use the activities at the end of each chapter and the activities and the sample exam on the course website. Remember to periodically review the

preceding chapters as well.

Chapter 7: Outline

(Italicized words are key terms.)

I.   Communication fosters interpersonal relationships but there are influences affecting our choices.
   A.   Appearance and complementary needs are factors in establishing closer relationships with others, as we tend to like people similar to us.
   B.   We are attracted to people who like us and we appreciate competent people. Self-disclosure increases liking, as does proximity.

II.   Dyadic communication is *contextually interpersonal*; but treating one another as unique individuals makes it *qualitatively interpersonal*.
   A.   Scarcity of qualitatively interpersonal interactions contributes to their
           value.
   B.   Relationships can be enhanced by mediated communication; but when personal face-to-face interaction commences, the majority of these relationships are terminated.

III.   Virtually every verbal statement contains a *content message* and a *relational message*.
   A.   Content focuses on the subject, while relational indicates feelings.
   B.   *Affinity*, *respect*, *immediacy*, and *control* can affect relational messages by adding or subtracting dimensions.
   C.   *Metacommunication*, the messages we send referring to other messages, involves analysis and should be used carefully.

IV.   A *developmental model* of the rise and fall of relationships shows how these connections are formed and fall apart.
   A.   Relationships commence with an initial stage and come together via experimenting, intensifying, integrating, and bonding.
   B.   When the individuals involved seek to reestablish their separate identities, the process of differentiating is occurring. That can lead to circumscribing, stagnating, avoiding, and eventually terminating actions. Then the relationship is over.

 V. Communicators seek important goals through all relationships in a
        dialectical model suggesting simultaneous *dialectical tensions*.
     A. Seeking involvement without sacrificing identity exemplifies the connection versus autonomy tension.
     B. Wanting stability without staleness reflects the predictability versus novelty tension.
     C. The desire for openness versus the need for privacy creates a tension.
     D. Managing the dialectical tensions presents challenges. Strategies include denial, disorientation, selection, alternation, segmentation,

moderation, reframing, and reaffirmation.
VI.   Our communication is affected by the conflicting drives for *intimacy versus distance*.
    A. Intimacy can be simply defined as closeness. Shared physical and intellectual activities and shared emotions are ways we use to get close to another person.
    B. Women are more willing than men to share their thoughts and feelings.
    C. Men grow close by doing things together.
    D. Collectivist and individualistic cultures vary in degrees of *self-disclosure* and personal familiarity.
VII. Self-disclosure is the process of deliberately revealing about oneself information that is significant and would not normally have been known by others.
    A. *Social penetration models* of self-disclosure involve *breadth* and *depth*.
    B. The *Johari Window* model represents self-awareness and the relational quality of knowledge about you from others.
    C. Self-disclosure is influenced by culture, usually occurs in dyads, is usually symmetrical, occurs incrementally, and is relatively scarce.
VIII. There are guidelines for the appropriate expression of self-disclosure.
    A. Is the other person important to you, and is the contemplated disclosure worth the risk?
    B. Is the amount and type appropriate and relevant to the situation?
    C. Will the self-disclosure be reciprocated, understood, and beneficial for both?
IX.   Although honesty is desirable, we often are not completely truthful at times of discomfort.
    A. *Altruistic lies* are sometimes considered helpful.
    B. *Equivocal language* often is used to avoid unpleasantness.
    C. Hints are more direct but involve relational messages that can be missed.

Chapter 7: Summary

Sometimes the options concerning our relationships are limited. At other times we actively seek out or attempt to avoid relationships. The way the other person looks is a factor, although the importance of physical attractiveness diminishes as the relationship progresses. We tend to like people similar to us; but differences help a relationship, provided they are complementary. We are interested in establishing relationships complementary to self, provided we do not look bad by comparison. Appropriate revelations shared via disclosure can build on the possibility of liking, and proximity allows us to gather more information for our decision.

We take all these influences and often unconsciously balance them through the social exchange theory. Whether we get positive feedback or not influences our decision to form and maintain relationships.

All dyadic communication is contextually interpersonal communication. Yet context is not always an accurate gauge of connectivity. If quality is preferred over quantity and we treat the other person as unique, then we are engaged in qualitatively interpersonal communication. Research confirms that computer-mediated communication can enhance quantity and quality more rapidly than the face-to-face form because of the anonymity of online interactions. When personal face-to-face interaction commences, the majority of relationships that were initiated online are terminated.

Virtually every verbal statement contains messages of two kinds: content messages focus on the actual subject and words, whereas relational messages express feelings, attitudes, and opinions. Relational messages involve affinity, the degree to which we like or appreciate another, as well as respect, admiration, and esteem. *Metacommunication* is the term used to describe the messages inside a message that refer to other messages.

Communication within either personal or romantic relationships often is described via a developmental model that runs from coming together or falling apart. All relationships begin with an initial contact. The next stage is experimentation. If the relationship develops toward an expression of support, the intensification promotes directly expressed feelings. When "we" start sharing commitments, the relationship is integrating. Usually what follows is a symbolic gesture or demonstration of the import of the relationship. This bonding can be in the form of a business contract, an initiation rite, or a public display or declaration of exclusivity. These are the stages of relationships coming together.

Once the communicators have formed this commonality, they sometimes have the need to reestablish individual identities. The differentiating need for autonomy is not always negative. When restrictions and restraints cause withdrawal or avoidance, leading to shrinking interest and lagging commitment, the relationship has entered the circumscribing stage. After that, the relationship begins to stagnate. If stagnation becomes too unpleasant, parties begin to separate themselves by avoiding each other. Usually there is only one more stage of falling apart, and that is termination. The relationship is then over.

The building and then eventual deterioration of a relationship is neither always progressive nor ultimately inevitable. Challenges exist both in a brand-new or a decades-long relationship as the partners struggle to balance dialectical tensions of opposing or incompatible forces. When a person is balancing the desire to make a connection versus the desire to remain autonomous, there is tension. Stability is an important need in a relationship; but familiarity can lead to boredom and stagnation. The dialectic of predictability versus novelty reflects this tension. Yet, along with the need for intimacy, we may have an equally important need to disengage. These sometimes conflicting drives create the openness-versus-privacy dialectic. There is a measurable pattern of fluctuation between disclosure and privacy in every stage of a relationship.

There are a number of strategies by which these challenges can be managed. One of the least functional is denial. In the strategy of selection, sometimes a communicator responds to one end of the dialectical spectrum and ignores the other. At times people use a strategy called alteration—swinging from one extreme to the other. Another tactic is segmentation, the compartmentalizing of different areas of the relationship. A preferred option is moderation, or compromising between the extremes. Other communicators might use reframing, a redefinition that causes the apparent contradiction to disappear. The most difficult yet most productive strategy is reaffirmation. Acknowledging that tensions will never disappear, and embracing the challenge, is a formidable task; but it keeps growth present.

The key element in most relationships is closeness. That is the basic definition of intimacy. The desire for physical intimacy begins before birth and continues into adulthood. Intellectual sharing also is a form of intimacy. An exchange of ideas brings communicators within range of strong relational bonds. A third quality of intimacy is emotion: exchanging important feelings. Closeness to others through shared activities provides the basis for growth and development of relationships. Not even the strongest relationships operate all four levels of intimacy at the highest level at all times.

Differences exist in how the genders display intimacy. As a group, women share emotional intimacy more than men. Men grow close to one another by doing things together. Culture influences intimacy between communicators. Collectivist and individualistic cultures contrast in formality of emotional and physical closeness.

We find others more attractive, and are more inclined toward qualitative interpersonal relationships, when private information is shared. The process of deliberately revealing information about our self that is significant and would not normally be known is called self-disclosure. A social penetration model of self-disclosure involves the breadth of information volunteered, the range of subjects being discussed, and the depth or shift from nonrevealing to personal. Another model representing how self-disclosure works is the Johari Window.

The use of self-disclosure requires understanding of how the process operates. It is influenced by culture; it usually occurs in dyads rather than groups; it is usually symmetrical; and because it occurs incrementally, it is relatively scarce. Before self-disclosing, you internally ask the following guiding questions. Is the other person important? Is the risk reasonable? Is the amount and type of self-disclosure appropriate? Is the self-disclosure relevant? Will there be reciprocation? Will the effect be constructive? Will the self-disclosure be clear and understandable?

Although honesty is desirable in principle, it often carries risk, with potentially unpleasant consequences. Three common alternatives to self-disclosure are lies, equivocation, and hinting. Altruistic lies are seen as harmless and sometimes helpful but, when discovered, can be traumatic to the person lied to. Equivocal language, often used to avoid unpleasantness or embarrassment, can cause confusion. A hint is more direct than equivocal language and is aimed at getting a desired response. The challenge of establishing unique and satisfactory interpersonal relationships hinges on the effectiveness and appropriateness with which trustworthy, clear, and understandable self-disclosures have been made.

Chapter 7: Key Terms

For each of these terms, define the term, give an example, and explain the significance of the term.

1. affinity

2. altruistic lies

3. breadth

4. content message

5. contextually interpersonal communication

6. depth

7. developmental models

8. dialectical model

9. dialectical tensions

10. equivocal language

11. immediacy

12. intimacy

13. Johari Window

14.   metacommunication

15.   qualitatively interpersonal communication

16.   relational message

17.   respect

18.   self-disclosure

19.   social penetration model

Chapter 7: Review Questions

These questions are designed to help you understand this chapter's concepts and express your understanding in your own words. For practice with true/false and multiple- choice questions, use the course website.

1. Identify the ten stages of the developmental model according to which relationships come together and fall apart.

2. What are the dialectical tensions present in most relationships?

3. There are four types of intimacy. Identify them and give an example of each.
4. What factors guide whether you will or will not self-disclose?

5. Oscar and Macon are shooting hoops when Lidia walks by. Macon and Lidia are lab partners in biology, so he calls for her to come over. Oscar snaps at Macon to stop fooling around and pay attention to the game. Lidia is offended by Oscar's rudeness and hurries away. This is an example of what?

_____ bonding, circumscribing, and termination

_____ gender differences in self-disclosure

_____ denial, disorientation, selection, and moderation

_____ lies, equivocation, and hinting

_____ several types of intimacy

6. Denim leans close and in a soft tone tells you his parents are getting a divorce. Denim says that the situation would be less stressful if he had confidence that any of his so-called friends really cared. Denim stops talking and makes direct eye contact. Why are you uncomfortable?

_____ Denim is a man and men should not talk about feelings

_____ Denim is experimenting where you want integration

_____ Denim's relational message is seeking reciprocation

_____ you closed your Johari Window

_____ your culture does not approve of divorce

Chapter 7: Thinking Outside the Box: Synthesizing Your Knowledge

These questions are designed to help you develop the big picture by blending what you've learned in this chapter and elsewhere.

1. Recall the closest, best friend you had in the third grade. Is that person still, today, your closest, best friend? What influenced your choice of that friend back in the third grade? Look at the developmental model of the stages of relationships and identify the stage of this "friendship" today. Explain.

2. When was the last time you used an alternative to appropriate self-disclosure with a friend or loved one? Defend your ethical justification.

Chapter 7: Answers to Review Questions

Your answers should include the following:

1. *In the developmental model of the stages of relationships, a relationship starts coming together with initiating and progresses to experimenting, intensifying, integrating, and bonding. Relationships are said to be falling apart if they move from differentiating to circumscribing and then stagnating, avoiding, and terminating.*

2. *Communicators who are trying to balance dialectical tensions of certain incompatible goals look for a median between several dyads: connection versus autonomy, predictability versus novelty,*

and openness versus privacy.

3.   *Physical intimacy could be expressed by sitting close to someone in the cafeteria. An example of intellectual intimacy could be any exchange of important ideas with another, as in debating the merits of purchasing a hybrid car instead of using public transportation. Emotional intimacy is displayed, for instance, by friends sharing thoughts and feelings at a funeral. Shared activities bring you closer when you and others are working side by side, or on a team or committee, and shared experiences result.*

4.   *Before self-disclosing, you quickly run through a mental checklist of qualifiers. Is this disclosure culturally acceptable? Is the other person important enough to you to justify the act? Is the risk reasonable, or is the possibility of rejection too great? What amount and type of disclosure is appropriate? Is the information you are considering revealing relevant to the situation? Will the disclosure be reciprocated? Will the effect be constructive of sharing? Is the disclosure clear and understandable? If any of these meet a negative reply, you usually exercise restraint.*

5.   *Oscar and Macon are sharing a physical activity, and Macon feels an intellectual connection with Lidia. The rudeness between Oscar and Lidia, while unpleasant, is a form of emotional intimacy. So the correct answer to this question is that several forms of intimacy are on display.*

6.   *Denim's language, both verbal and nonverbal, is communicating a relational message seeking reciprocation.*

Chapter 7: Answers to Thinking Outside the Box

1.   *Appearance, similarity, complementary characteristics, reciprocal attraction, competence, disclosure, and proximity all contribute to our selection of a close best friend, even in the third grade. Although the social exchange theory might not be as obvious at that age, we still balance cost versus rewards. Time, maturity, situations, environment, and interests likely have contributed to the movement of the relationship from bonding to another stage of the developmental model. Indications are that the longer the period of time that has elapsed since the third grade, the more likely that you have terminated your interpersonal relationship with your childhood close best friend.*

2. *We are sensitive to embarrassment, uncomfortable and awkward situations, and the feelings of others. Even the most well-intentioned communicator accepts that in certain situations, complete and blunt honesty is not the best policy. A brief jog of your memory of activities from just the past three days will bring up instances of lies, equivocation, and hinting.*

CHAPTER 8:
IMPROVING INTERPERSONAL RELATIONSHIPS

SQ3R in Action:

Generate an SQ3R chart for this chapter here:
http://www.teach-nology.com/web_tools/graphic_org/sq3r

Survey

Skim the title, Chapter Highlights, objectives ("You should understand" and "You should be able to"), headings, tables, photos, cartoons, figures, charts, and items in the margin. Glance at the titles of the Critical Thinking Probes and Ethical Challenges. At the end of each chapter, look over the list of Key Terms, Activities, and Resources.

Question

Ask yourself questions. What do you know about these topics from your own life experiences and from other classes? Ask these six questions in each section: who, what, when, where, how, and why.

Read

Take one heading at a time and read to find the answers to the questions you've posed.

Recite

In your own words, say the answer aloud and then write it out.

Review

Review each section and then review the whole chapter. This is a good time to use the activities at the end of each chapter and the activities and the sample exam on the course website. Remember to periodically review the

preceding chapters as well.

Chapter 8: Outline

(Italicized words are key terms.)

I.   Every communication relationship has a feeling, a mood, an emotional tone referred to as *communication climate*.
    A.   Positive confirming messages verify value, increasing recognition, acknowledgment, and endorsement.
    B.   *Disconfirming* messages deny value via disagreement, aggression, rejection, disputing, ignoring, or disregarding.
    C.   Communication climates take on a life of their own either in positive reinforcement or negative *escalatory* conflict *spirals*. *Avoidance spirals* can also be destructive.

II.   The *Gibb categories*, contrasting defense-arousing versus actions aimed at reducing a threat, can create increasingly positive or negative climates.
    A.   One challenge is *evaluative* communication, *"you" language*, against descriptive communication, *"I" language*.
    B.   Another compares a *controlling* message versus problem orientation, and behavior manipulation *strategy* versus honest spontaneity.
    C.   *Neutrality* indicates indifference, whereas *empathy* implies acceptance of feelings.
    D.   *Superiority* triggers defensiveness, whereas *equality* signals worth; and *certainty* is unyielding, in contrast to *provisionalism,* which introduces and acknowledges practical considerations.

III.   Communication *conflicts* arise in all relationships as an expressed struggle between at least two parties who perceive incompatible goals, scarce rewards, and interference from the other parties as they seek to achieve their goals.
    A.   Conflict is expressed via *nonassertion*, *direct aggression*, *passive aggression*, *indirect communication*, and *assertion*.
    B.   A complete assertive message, the most effective response, includes behavioral *description*, interpretation, description of feelings, description of consequences, and statement of intentions.
    C.   Gender influences and cultural attitudes are reflected in our approach to conflict.
    D.   Computer-mediated communication fosters conflict through use of delay, disinhibition, and permanence.

IV.   The resolution of conflicts has four possible outcomes: *win–lose, lose–lose problem solving, compromise*, and *win–win problem solving*.
    A.   Win–win is the solution that satisfies the needs of everyone involved.
    B.   Win–win requires the following steps: identify your problem and

unmet needs, make a date, describe your problem and needs, check back with your partner, solicit partner's needs, check understanding, negotiate, and follow up.

Chapter 8: Summary

Every relationship has a feeling, a pervasive mood, coloring the interactions of the participants. This communication climate, the emotional tone of the relationship, is determined by the degree to which participants see themselves as valued. Confirming messages signal worth with positive levels of recognition, acknowledgment, and endorsement. Disconfirming messages deny value, not ony through disagreement but also by means of aggressive rejection, disregard of the other, purposeful actions to ignore, and attitudes perceived as hurtful. Once climates have formed, they grow in a self-perpetuating spiral, either positive or negative. In escalatory conflict spirals, parties use disconfirming messages to reinforce one another. Avoidance spirals are destructive to a relationship because as they gradually lessen in intensity, the parties become less dependent on each other, inevitably withdrawing their investment in the relationship.

The Gibb categories of six types of defense-arousing communication versus six contrasting types aimed at reducing threat and defensiveness show choices in creating and maintaining positive or negative climates. Defense-provoking evaluation with "you" language is in contrast to descriptive communication using "I" language. A controlling attitude imposes a solution, whereas a problem orientation avoids declared winners and seeks shared accomplishment. A poor communication climate is created when strategy is used to manipulate. The opposite of a manipulative climate is characterized by spontaneity or straightforward honesty. Neutrality can arouse defensiveness because it signals indifference. Empathy, on the other hand, confirms acceptance of the other person's feelings. Any indication of superiority generates defensiveness, which can be lessened by conveying an attitude of equality. Dogmatic, unyielding certainty is resisted, whereas a provisional acknowledgment of the opinions of others is perceived as reasonable.

It is impossible to avoid communication conflict, an expressed struggle between at least two interdependent parties who perceive incompatible goals, scarce rewards, and interference from the other parties in their efforts to achieve their respective goals. One of the ways conflict is expressed is through nonassertion, the inability or unwillingness to express thoughts. The opposite of nonassertion is the directly aggressive message that is conducive to confrontation. Passive aggression, though more subtle, still reflects opposition. Indirect communication takes a roundabout course to deliver a message of disagreement without arousing hostility. Too often, indirection is interpreted as vague or oblique hinting, lacking clarity. When people handle conflict by expressing their needs, thoughts, and feelings directly and respectfully, they are being assertive. Assertion does not guarantee success, but it has the best chance of satisfaction over the other expressed responses.

A complete assertive message has five parts: behavioral description, your interpretation of the other's behavior, a description of your feelings, a description of the consequences of the behavior, and a statement of your intentions. These elements do not have to be presented in the order listed, nor is it necessary to separate them into individualized components. The important thing to remember is that you have not communicated effectively until the receiver understands everything you have said. Both patience and persistence are essential in the successful delivery of assertive communication.

Gender differences when dealing with communication conflict first appear when young boys issue orders and young girls suggest solutions. This pattern typically continues into adulthood. As a general rule, women are more likely to use indirect strategies instead of confronting matters head-on. Men are more likely to use aggressive approaches to get their way. However, recent observations have indicated that females tend to be more assertive when expressing their ideas in terms of feelings, as males withdraw from such discussion.

Computer-mediated communication has changed interpersonal communication approaches and conflict expression because of the inherent delay between sending and responding. The absence of face-to-face immediacy has contributed to disinhibition when a communication partner might otherwise be considering consequences. The other factor affecting the development of conflict in the social media is existence of a permanent transcript, which of course is not a feature of face-to-face dialogue. A record or chronicle of exchanges can clear up misunderstandings, but reviewing transcripts can also renew emotions and perpetuate an escalatory conflict spiral.

Individualistic cultures look at assertiveness and even aggression differently than collectivist cultures. Appropriate, admirable behavior in one culture is considered rude and insensitive in another. A high-context communication style emphasizes harmony within the group over a low-context style of speaking directly without ambiguity.

No matter the style, culture, or gender, every conflict is a struggle to have one's goals met. The outcome or end result of communication conflict is often expressed in terms indicating success or failure. In win–lose conflict resolution, one party achieves success at the expense of the other. Lose–lose problem solving results in neither side's being satisfied by the outcome. With compromise, both parties get at least some of what they wanted, though both sacrifice some of their goals. Win–win problem solving aspires to find a solution that satisfies the needs of everyone involved. This often entails some compromises, achieved only when the parties work together toward a mutually satisfying outcome.

Although win–win is often most desirable, it is one of the hardest outcomes to achieve. Chances of success are increased if the parties approach the conflict with the following procedures in mind. Identify your problem and unmet needs. Use descriptive rather than evaluative language to make the problem yours; and then clarify what it is you want. Make a date; but bear in mind that scheduling a meeting "now" will not always be advantageous or convenient. Describe your problem and needs, using "I" language. Then check back with your communication partner. Understanding achieved through clarification prompts positive responses far more frequently than does confusion that parties have neglected to eliminate. Solicit your partner's needs. Make your position clear, and then listen to comprehend and understand, being sure to check your understanding of your partner's needs with the person himself or herself. Paraphrase or ask questions for clarity. Negotiate a solution. Consider options, choices, and alternatives. Evaluate the possibilities. Decide on a solution that looks best for all concerned. Follow up on the solution. You cannot determine with certainty that a given choice is the best until it has been tried. Perhaps a review or reevaluation of the solution is necessary after a time to keep on top of the problem, to continue to use creativity to solve it. Not all conflicts can end in win–win; but they can still generate goodwill if handled respectfully, with a genuine desire to improve the relationship.

Chapter 8: Key Terms

For each of these terms, define the term, give an example, and explain the significance of the term.

1. assertive communication

2. avoidance conflict spiral

3. certainty

4. communication conflict

5. compromise

6. conflict

7. controlling communication

8. description

9. direct aggression

10. disconfirming response

11.   empathy

12.   equality

13.   escalatory spiral

14.   evaluative communication

15.   Gibb categories

16.   "I" language

17.   indirect communication

18.   lose–lose problem solving

19.   neutrality

20.   nonassertion

21.   passive aggression

22.   problem orientation

23.   provisionalism

24.   spiral

25.   strategy

26.   superiority

27.   win–lose problem solving

28.   win–win problem solving

29.   "you" language

Chapter 8: Review Questions

These questions are designed to help you understand this chapter's concepts and express your understanding in your own words. For practice with true/false and multiple- choice questions, use the course website.

1.   A companion wants to accomplish a set of goals that are the mirror-image opposite of your goals. Using the material from this chapter as a reference, explain how you can prevent an escalatory conflict spiral.

2.   Explain the different responses possible in a communication conflict, giving examples.

3.   Detail the options possible as an outcome in a conflict. Why are two unacceptable and two others preferred?

4.   As you are driving along the highway with family members as passengers, a communication conflict grows in intensity. Your mother urges
you to slow down and be more careful; your father demands that you get in a different lane and blast your horn as you pass the slowpokes; and your older brother insists that he should have been driving all along. How can you respond and not make matters worse?

_____ overpower the others with "you" language

_____ be assertive and seek possible compromise

_____ stop the car and kick the complainers out

_____ use more direct aggression to strengthen your points

_____ realize that nonassertion is your only course of action

Chapter 8: Thinking Outside the Box: Synthesizing Your Knowledge

These questions are designed to help you develop the big picture by blending what you've learned in this chapter and elsewhere.

1.   Your study group has six members. Two obviously speak English as a second language, a third has never spoken up in class, and two others sees more interested in flirting than studying. You have nothing in common with anyone else in the group; but the project is due by the next class session. In the turmoil, you interject an assertive message. Explain the procedures you chose.

2.   You take an object back to the store for a refund. Well aware that you do not have the receipt, you expect resistance in achieving

your goal. After all, the store is operating to make a profit, not to give money away. What outcome should you realistically expect, and how can you achieve it?

Chapter 8: Answers to Review Questions

Your answers should include the following:

1. *You and your companion are experiencing a communication conflict, and the climate could build into a negative escalatory spiral if statements, opinions, and needs are expressed with evaluation communication using "you" language, which will be perceived as accusatory and judgmental. Descriptive communication uses "I" language and makes the interaction personal and about your feelings. Trying to control the choices or impose a resolution causes defensive feelings in the other. A better choice would be to seek problem orientation cohesiveness involving the "we" who are concerned about the situation. If the other thinks you are using a manipulative strategy, cooperation will be impossible. Careful, considerate honesty with a straightforward approach may not always succeed, but it often generates a positive, respectful climate. Indifference is disconfirming because it indicates a lack of concern. Empathy shows that you respect the other's feelings and are interested. Any signs or indicators of superiority from one partner will be met with defensive reaction by the other. Disagreement with an air of equality conveys worth and dignity. Try not to appear dogmatic, unyielding, or absolutely certain that your position is the only right one. Recognize that possibilities and choices exist, and acknowledge that there are positive, constructive options available, with emphasis on those supported by logical reasons.*

2. *Nonassertion signals the inability or unwillingness to express thoughts or feelings related to the conflict. Avoidance and accommodation will not resolve the conflict; rather, frustration will build and the conflict will continue. Direct aggression is confrontation and usually results in a reciprocal hostile response. Passive aggression is more subtle but still expresses hostility. Pseudoaccommodators pretend agreement but do not comply. Guiltmakers seek control by manipulation. Jokers avoid the issues by using humor to hide disagreement. Trivial tyrannizers nitpick and complain in tiny doses of confrontation. There are those who conveniently forget and those who withhold valuable information to punish and generate a feeling of payback. Indirect communication conveys messages in a roundabout manner. Hinting sometimes*

saves face and softens the blow, but it is still often too oblique for most people to understand. Assertive people communicate directly and respectfully, stating feelings, thoughts, needs, and goals clearly, without judgment of others or dictatorial conditions.

3.   *One of the most common outcomes in a communication conflict is lose–lose. In this situation, one party achieves its goal at the expense of the other. Since no one likes being the loser, it often happens that both parties are so focused on winning that they refuse to allow other options to be considered, which means that both lose; that is, neither side is satisfied with the outcome. In another outcome, compromise, both sides gain something to consider as an achievement, while some sacrifice might be made. Partial satisfaction is preferred to no satisfaction. The best outcome, although rare and difficult to achieve, is win—win. If both parties feel satisfied, even though there has been compromise, the outcome can be called win—win.*

4.   *The person operating the car is responsible for final decisions and actions. Delivering an assertive message while seeking compromise allows all parties involved to understand the feelings, needs, and goals of the others. This approach will succeed, however, only if used with a respectful directness paired with willingness to listen and reciprocate with confirming messages.*

Chapter 8: Answers to Thinking Outside the Box

1.   *The gender and cultural differences in the group require awareness and acceptance of different communication styles. While being direct with respect is considered admirable in an individualistically oriented society, you must take care not to be perceived as manipulative or as ordering people around. Sensitivity to context should facilitate the empathetic delivery of an assertive message. Structure your message by reviewing objectively the behavior in question and your interpretation of another's behavior as it relates to the desired solution. Make it personal. Describe your feelings using "I" language. Then, without making accusations, explain what happens as a result of the behavior you have described. Explain the consequences in terms of what happens to you, what happens to the target of your message, and what happens to others. Clearly but respectfully state your intentions. Be aware of different listening styles and possible misinterpretations of your message. In communication, as in many other activities, patience and persistence are essential.*

2. *Realistically, compromise is the best outcome to expect. Partial satisfaction might include an exchange or a store credit. You want to maintain the relationship, which means you want to continue doing business at the store; so rather than holding out for a total refund, you should be open to giving up a part of your goal for the sake of getting something for your money. Store management does not want to lose either money or a customer; and so a settlement of something is preferred to nothing. "Get out and never come back" will benefit no one; nor will "I'll never shop here again." With compromise, both parties feel that the giving represented equal sacrifices and the getting was mutually satisfying.*

CHAPTER 9: COMMUNICATING IN GROUPS

SQ3R in Action:

Generate an SQ3R chart for this chapter here:
http://www.teach-nology.com/web_tools/graphic_org/sq3r

Survey

Skim the title, Chapter Highlights, objectives ("You should understand" and "You should be able to"), headings, tables, photos, cartoons, figures, charts, and items in the margin. Glance at the titles of the Critical Thinking Probes and Ethical Challenges. At the end of each chapter, look over the list of Key Terms, Activities, and Resources.

Question

Ask yourself questions. What do you know about these topics from your own life experiences and from other classes? Ask these six questions in each section: who, what, when, where, how, and why.

Read

Take one heading at a time and read to find the answers to the questions you've posed.

Recite

In your own words, say the answer aloud and then write it out.

Review

Review each section and then review the whole chapter. This is a good time to use the activities at the end of each chapter and the activities and the sample exam on the course website. Remember to periodically review the preceding chapters as well.

Chapter 9: Outline

(Italicized words are key terms.)

I.   A great deal of the information you have learned, the benefits your have gained, even your very identity, have come from *group* membership.
   A.   A group is defined as a small collection of people who interact with each other, usually face to face over time, in order to reach goals.
   B.   *Virtual groups*, which use mediated communication, meet more easily and more quickly than face-to-face groups and level status and gender differences faster.
   C.   Group members are motivated by *individual goals* as well as *group goals.*
   D.   Groups operate within a framework of common characteristics because of *explicit rules* and unstated *social*, *procedural*, and *task norms.*
   E.   *Roles* define patterns of behavior within a group. These can be *formal* or *informal task roles* and *social roles*; frequently, persons occupying *dysfunctional roles* prevent group effectiveness.
   F.   The interaction within a group could resemble an *all-channel network*, a *chain network*, or a *wheel network*. Success in a wheel network depends heavily on the skill of a *gatekeeper*.
II.   There are several approaches a group can use to make decisions. These include *consensus*, majority control, expert opinion, minority control, and authority rule.
   A.   *Individualistic* versus collectivist cultural approaches clash the most noticeably in a group setting.
   B.   *Power distance* and *uncertainty avoidance* are also cultural factors that play a role in decision making.
   C.   Some cultures stress task orientation; and others have a high degree of social orientation.
   D.   Members of some cultures seek short-term, quick payoffs; others defer gratification in pursuit of long-term goals.
III.   All groups have a leader or leaders, whether elected, designated, or assumed.
   A.   *Power* is defined as the ability to influence others.
   B.   The ability to influence others can be in the form of *legitimate power*, the power held by a *nominal leader, coercive power, reward power, expert power, information power*, or *referent power.*
   C.   *Trait theories of leadership* incorporate social, goal-related and physical appearance skills, as well as intelligence and dependability,
   E.   Groups are managed by means of an *authoritarian leadership style*, a democratic leadership style, the *laissez-faire leadership* style, or *situational leadership.*

Chapter 9: Summary

A great deal of the information you have learned, the benefits you have gained—even your identity—have come from group membership. A group consists of a small collection of people who interact with one another, usually face to face over time, in order to reach goals. In groups, members do not just interact; they are interdependent. Duration of time spent together contributes to a sense of group identity and history. There is no arbitrary limit on the size of an effective group; usually, however, bigness exacerbates communication difficulties. Virtual groups using mediated communication have an advantage in convenience and time; in addition, the status and gender differences of group members are not as heavily weighted.

The most obvious reason for a person to join a group is to accomplish an individual goal. Group goals can be a motivation to be in a group. There is strength in numbers. Some individuals might conceal a hidden agenda for participating in a group. As long as the members' goals align, the effectiveness of the group is not damaged.

Many groups have explicit rules. These are officially stated guidelines. Alongside the official rules, unstated norms regulate policy and procedure. Social norms govern the relationships between members. Procedural norms outline operational acceptance; and task norms focus on how goals are to be obtained. Within the group there are patterns of behavior defined as roles. Formal roles are assigned, whereas informal, or functional, roles exist in which members execute functions outside their delineated formal positions. Task roles help the group accomplish goals; and social roles, sometimes called maintenance roles, help relationships between the members progress smoothly. Too often a member's role will be a dysfunctional one, thus preventing group effectiveness. As the time spent together increases, members will make bids for certain roles. The three most common role-related problems are unfilled task or social roles, an absence of candidates to fill needed roles, and role fixation despite a lacki of competence.

The physical arrangement of the meeting space influences the effectiveness of group communication. A circular table increases the flow of participation, while a rectangular working area lessens it. Members staying together and sharing every piece of information interact in an all-channel network. Irregular, nonimmediate contact, one to another, represents a chain network. Sequential movement from one member to another follows the model of the wheel network. The success or failure of a wheel network depends heavily on the skill of a gatekeeper, the person through whom the information flows.

The method groups used to reach decisions often defines group identity. Consensus occurs when all members of a group support a decision. With all members agreeing, the commitment of the group is solidified. Consensus takes time to build, however, and emotions can be heightened if compromise is not forthcoming. Majority control is advantageous because it indicates that at least 51 percent of the members are in agreement; but it too often makes the 49 percent feel inferior, hence likely to decrease their participation. Expert opinion can be immediate and beneficial if the expert's advice has credibility. Minority control, in which a few members decide for the entire group, is usually observed in larger groups—for example, a board of directors of a large corporation or an executive committee of a national political party. Authority rule is often used the most by autocratic leaders. It has the advantage of producing quick decisions; but there is the disadvantage of problems that result when the other members come to believe that their contribution is deemed useless or unnecessary.

Increasing diversity at school, work, and play changes the traditional ethnic and cultural homogeneity of groups. Five cultural forces shape the attitudes and behaviors of groups and individuals. Group members today must contend with individualistic primary responsibility to self, which is to be balanced with collectivistic feelings of loyalty and obligation to the group. Some cultures accept power distance in status, privilege, age, experience, and training, whereas others acknowledge such distinctions grudgingly while expecting consideration and equal treatment. Some group members might welcome and accept risk while their fellow group members might dislike surprises and ambiguity. The movement toward or away from uncertainty avoidance determines the leadership style found most favorable. Cultures characterized by strong task orientation rely on getting the job done; social orientation cultures are more likely to be concerned about feelings and team cohesiveness. Members of some cultures look for quick payoffs in the form of immediate results,whereas members of other cultures are willing to defer gratification in pursuit of long-term goals. Cultural differences do not account for every communication conflict in group functions; but recognizing such variations can enable the group to be achieve better internal communications.

Even in groups without a designated leader or leaders, some members will have more influence than others. Power is defined as the ability to influence others. Legitimate power arises from the title one holds. The person officially labeled as being in charge is the nominal leader. Yet there are other means of influence. Coercive power comes from the threat or actual imposition of unpleasant consequences. Reward power lasts only as long as influence can be achieved by granting or promising desirable consequences. Expert power comes from people influencing the others by what they know or can do. Information power accrues to the person with the knowledge to help the group reach its goal. Referent power comes from others'respect, liking, and trust for a given member.

Trait theories of leadership identify characteristics of power. Leaders tend to talk more fluently and to exhibit more social skills. They have more goal-related values, are usually intelligent, possess task-relevant information, and are seen as dependable. In addition, they are perceived as being physically more attractive. Because these traits are subjective, a more definitive measure of leadership rests in communication style. An authoritarian leader relies on legitimate, coercive, and reward power to influence others. A democratic leader invites participation and sharing in decision making. The laissez-faire leader gives up the power to dictate, transforming the group into a collection of equals. While each leadership style can produce acceptable results, research shows that a democratic approach correlates highly with success. Usually the best style of leadership is flexible enough to vary from one set of circumstances to the other. The "situational" leader must be sensitive to the readiness of the group's degree of motivation and willingness to be led.

Chapter 9: Key Terms

For each of these terms, define the term, give an example, and explain the significance of the term.

1.   all-channel network

2.   authoritarian leadership style

3.   chain network

4.   coercive power

5.   consensus

6.   democratic leadership style

7.   dysfunctional roles

8.   expert power

9.   formal role

10.   gatekeepers

11.   group

12.   group goals

13.   hidden agendas

14.   individual goals

15. individualistic orientation

16. informal roles

17. information power

18. laissez-faire leadership style

19. leadership grid

20. legitimate power

21. nominal leader

22. norms

23. power

24. power distance

25. procedural norms

26. referent power

27. reward power

28. roles

29. rule

30. situational leadership

31. social norms

32. social orientation

33. social roles

34. sociogram

35. task norms

36. task roles

37. trait theories of leadership

38.   uncertainty avoidance

39.   wheel network

40.   virtual groups

Chapter 9: Review Questions

These questions are designed to help you understand this chapter's concepts and express your understanding in your own words. For practice with true/false and multiple- choice questions, use the course website.

1. Identify a group you belong to and list three or four explicit rules. Then explain three or four norms this group also expects from members.

2. Explain the advantages and disadvantages of group decision-making methods.

3. Define power, and list examples of the different uses of power as discussed in the text.

4. Demetri, Greg, Wang, Maria, and Lars are in a group responsible for setting rules for student discipline in the classroom. The five always meet at the same table in the cafeteria, Wang takes lots of notes but never speaks up. Maria seems passive and meek and never argues. Demetri and Greg are both loud and sure of themselves. Lars just wants everyone to get along. What obvious challenges are obstacles to the group in accomplishing its goal?

_____ until the group elects a leader, nothing will be accomplished

_____ as the sole female in the group, Maria should take the notes

_____ Lars needs to be less dysfunctional

_____ according to the wheel network, Wang should be the nominal leader

_____ members need to recognize and adjust to cultural and gender attitudes

Chapter 9: Thinking Outside the Box: Synthesizing Your Knowledge

These questions are designed to help you develop the big picture by blending what you've learned in this chapter and elsewhere.

1. Select a group of which you are a member. Now think about the leader. What traits or unique communication-related characteristics does this person possess that make him or her an effective leader?

2. How do you know the association you have with others is or is not a group? Define and explain your answer.

Chapter 9: Answers to Review Questions

Your answers should include the following:

1. *Many groups, from activity organizations or extracurricular school groups or participation units, have a set of explicit rules. These may be in the form of a charter or constitution or clearly stated policy and procedure. Official rules could contain parameters for or against smoking, eligibility for membership, acceptable behavior or dress code, parking, standards for dealing with absences or tardiness, meeting etiquette, and even allowable choices of recreation and pleasure. Norms, on the other hand, are understood and accepted but not normally of interest if no one is violating them. Norms might include shared values, beliefs, behaviors, and procedures for social acceptance. Norms might also focus on responsibility and job achievement outside the realm of orders or instruction—for example, who can or cannot issue those instructions.*

2. *Consensus has full participation and agreement but cannot be reached without the expenditure of time and the will to compromise. In some instances, there is neither time nor willingness to compromise. In majority control, at least 51 percent of the members are in agreement, but the others, perhaps as numerous as 49 percent, are likely to be left behind, disgruntled and feeling ineffective. Expert opinion is efficient and convenient only if the declared expert has the credibility necessary to secure the respect of all in the group. Minority control saves time because fewer people are involved n the decision-making process, but communication is diffused through impersonal channels. Authority rule leads to quick decisions and avoids confrontation, but its effectiveness is diminished if group members feel disregarded or unnecessary.*

3. *Power is defined as the ability to influence others. Legitimate power arises when one has the title of nominal leader, be it elected, appointed, or*

assumed. For example, the person directing traffic in a construction zone might have been elected or appointed or might simply have decided without prompting to assume the responsibility. Coercive power uses intimidation or threat of unpleasant consequences. "Give me your lunch money or I will beat you up" typifies coercive influence. Reward power promises privileges or incentives. You could be influenced to behave at the doctor's office with the promise of ice cream later. Expert power exists when members accept another's qualifications, such as the operating room staff acknowledging the expertise of the surgeon. Information power comes from knowledge: "I know my way around these streets, so I will give directions to the group." Referent power is perception. Respect, liking, and trust are elements of this influential power. Admiration is a factor in the choice to follow the lead of someone in the mall or to emulate a given trendsetter in fashion.

4. *Cultural and gender differences are in play, and the separate members need to recognize and adjust their attitudes in the interest of uniting as an effective group to accomplish their goal.*

Chapter 9: Answers to Thinking Outside the Box

1. *Most leaders want the role and act in a way that will help them achieve it. Upon examination of group dynamics, it is found that leaders tend to talk more often and more fluently. They are perceived as popular, cooperative, and skilled in social settings. Leaders usually are superior to rank-and-file group members in intelligence, and they tend to possess more task-related information.In addition to being dependable, leaders are seen as being more physically attractive than other members. This does not apply to all leaders, but the ones using democratic or laissez-faire styles often benefit from perceptions of personal charisma that overrule factual evidence. If the leader listens, the leader is perceived as wise. If the members agree enthusiastically with the leader's decision, the leader is said to have charisma. Effective leadership generates satisfaction; and members compliment themselves on their selection of the competent leader by attaching to the leader qualities they admire.*

2. *A group consists of a small collection of people who interact with each other, usually face to face over time, in order to reach goals. A collection of people gawking at the scene of an accident is not a group because the individuals are merely onlookers, they are not interacting interdependently. Spending time riding three floors in a crowded elevator does not qualify as belonging to a group because there is no sense of identity or history of participation. When it comes to groups, size does matter. It takes at least three to be a group. As for the maximum number, that is open to debate. However, when individuals cease to know and react to every other*

member, the group has become an organization and, by definition, no longer can be called a group. This becomes evident as increases in numbers makes it harder to schedule meetings, access information, communicate effectively, or encourage participation. Ease of scheduling, accessibility of information, and so on are necessary in a group. A sign that you and certain others are not in a group is failure of the other persons to share a goal or goals. Without shared goals, the individuals do not comprise a group. Individual goals can coincide with group goals; but there must be a shared destination. Groups usually have rules and always have norms. By not agreeing to the norms, one also does not agree to membership in the group. Although groups range in size and degree of involvement, the answer to this question essentially boils down to a simple formula: If you have to ask, odds are you are not in a group.

CHAPTER 10: SOLVING PROBLEMS IN GROUPS

SQ3R in Action:

Generate an SQ3R chart for this chapter here:
http://www.teach-nology.com/web_tools/graphic_org/sq3r

Survey

Skim the title, Chapter Highlights, objectives ("You should understand" and "You should be able to"), headings, tables, photos, cartoons, figures, charts, and items in the margin. Glance at the titles of the Critical Thinking Probes and Ethical Challenges. At the end of each chapter, look over the list of Key Terms, Activities, and Resources.

Question

Ask yourself questions. What do you know about these topics from your own life experiences and from other classes? Ask these six questions in each section: who, what, when, where, how, and why.

Read

Take one heading at a time and read to find the answers to the questions you've posed.

Recite

In your own words, say the answer aloud and then write it out.

Review

Review each section and then review the whole chapter. This is a good time to use the activities at the end of each chapter and the activities and the sample exam on the course website. Remember to periodically review the preceding chapters as well.

Chapter 10: Outline

(Italicized words are key terms.)

I.   The most common groups are learning, growth, social, and problem-solving.
      A.   A group offers more in the way of resources, accuracy, and commitment than are available to you are an individual.
      B.   Problem-solving groups are justified when the job is beyond the capacity of one person, individual tasks are interdependent, there is more than one possible decision or solution, and there is potential for disagreement.
II.   Groups adapt varied settings, reasons, and presentation styles to solve problems.
      A.   *Breakout groups, problem census, focus groups, parliamentary procedure* rules, *panel discussion, symposium,* and *forum* groups are some of the formats used to shape the ability to coordinate solutions.
      B.   Virtual groups are convenient for ease of scheduling, independence of participants, and anonymity-enhanced courage of contributors.
      C.   An effective problem-solving group uses a structured rational approach to identify the problem, analyze the problem, develop creative solutions, evaluate the solutions, implement the plan, and follow up.
      D.   Successful groups seem to follow a four-stage process consisting of *orientation stage, conflict stage, emergence stage,* and *reinforcement stage.*
III.   Groups are most effective when members have mutual respect and *cohesiveness.*
      A.   Cohesiveness and productivity are connected.
      B.   Cohesiveness is no guarantee of success, but it helps.
      C.   Group communication dangers to overcome include message *information underload* or *overload,* unequal participation, and pressure to conform to *groupthink.*

Chapter 10: Summary

      Groups come in many forms and use many styles to achieve their goals; but the
most common forms are learning, growth, social interaction and problem-solving. The process of solving problems in groups is not applied only when something is wrong; problem-solving groups are also used to meet challenges and perform tasks too complicated for an individual to handle. Groups have proved superior at

accomplishing a wide range of tasks because of the availability of more sources, the benefit of improved accuracy, and the participative decision-making commitment developed by group members and represented by the desire of all to contribute to resolving the situation that affects each member.

Not all situations justify using a group. If, however, the answer to the following questions is affirmative, then using a group to tackle a problem is warranted. Is the job beyond the capacity of one person? Are individuals' tasks interdependent? Is there more than one possible decision or solution? Is there potential for disagreement? Many jobs might be managed more quickly and efficiently by one person; but using the preceding questions as a yardstick will aid in selecting the best process for solving a given problem.

The structure of a group shapes its ability to achieve high-quality solutions. Breakout groups address an issue simultaneously and then report back to a mother group. Problem census separates issues from personalities. Focus groups do not include decision makers but, rather, report reactions and opinions to them. Groups following stilted parliamentary procedures may seem unnatural, but groups that use these rules in their format keep a discussion on track and allow all members to have a voice. Panel discussion groups talk over the topic and an audience eavesdrops. Symposium groups divide the topic into segments and each member contributes to the whole. A forum allows nonmembers to participate and is essentially audience driven. Virtual mediated communication groups have the advantage of easier scheduling and independent participation. A disadvantage is that the absence of nonverbal cues can mask or eradicate the emotional tone of communications. Virtual groups also eliminate almost all trace of spontaneity. It takes time to type a response. There is no one ideal way for groups to conduct their meetings, nor any single perfect format for accomplishing the tasks at hand.

Logic and reason usually play little part in how we make decisions. Feelings, social interaction, and preconceived assumptions contribute to nonrational decisions. Having a problem-solving structure in place is the best way to produce positive results. One model with flexibility for individual creativity yet formatted with a blueprint for continuity has six steps. Identify the problem and determine goals. Analyze the problem and identify supporting and restraining forces. Develop creative solutions through brainstorming or the nominal group technique. Brainstorming works only if members realize that criticism is forbidden, freewheeling is encouraged, quality is the objective, and members are expected to combine ideas and improve on them. A nominal group technique allows each member to work alone, later sharing in a round-robin fashion. The members then privately rank the choices and apply critical thinking to a discussion of the top ideas. Another step in the problem-solving process is to evaluate the solutions by asking which one or two best produces the desired results. Implement the plan. The final stage is one too often forgotten: follow up.

The group's charge is not completed until the progress of the decision has been gauged and revisions, if necessary, have been considered.

Once a group has interacted over time, a four-stage decision-making process unfolds. In the orientation stage members are tentative and cautious. The conflict stage involves the give-and-take of personal communication. Effective groups then enter the emergence stage as cooperation and compromise contribute to the search for a solution. Finally, an effective group reaches the reinforcement stage. Decisions are accepted and endorsed.

Once individuals within the group have bonded, achieving a collective sense of identity, they are said to have cohesiveness. Cohesiveness is defined as the degree to which members feel connected with and committed to their group. Eight factors contribute to cohesiveness in a group. They include group members having shared or compatible goals, progress being made toward those goals, and the sharing of norms and values by members in a way that doesn't cause individuals to feel that their status, dignity, or material or emotional well-being is threatened. When group members feel satisfied only with the help of other members, their interdependence contributes to cohesiveness. If there is a perceived threat from outside the group, cohesiveness increases. Mutual attraction and friendship assist in comfortable decision making, and members who have shared group experiences tend to draw together as a unit.

Even groups with the best intentions need to avoid several dangers if they are to achieve a satisfactory level of effectiveness. Information underload, an absence of adequate knowledge or research, can bog a group down. So too can information overload: an avalanche of data that overwhelms the processing of assimilating the material fairly and effectively. Unequal participation of group members with a poor balance of responsibilities or contributions tends to cause some members to withdraw. The tendency to go along to get along often results in bad decisions. If there is too much pressure on members to conform, the group as a whole adopts a groupthink mentality. This collective striving for unanimity discourages realistic appraisals of alternatives. Consensus is admirable, but "rocking the boat" can result in legitimate constructive reconsideration of what seems most popular. Rather than fostering accuracy, groupthink distorts reality.

Chapter 10: Key Terms

For each of these terms, define the term, give an example, and explain the significance of the term.

1.   brainstorming

2.   breakout groups

3.   cohesiveness

4.   conflict stage

5.   emergence stage

6.   focus group

7.   force field analysis

8.   forum

9.   groupthink

10.   information overload

11.   information underload

12.   nominal group technique

13.   orientation stage

14.   panel discussion

15.   parliamentary procedure

16.   participative decision making

17.   problem census

18.   reinforcement stage

19.   symposium

Chapter 10: Review Questions

These questions are designed to help you understand this chapter's concepts and express your understanding in your own words. For practice with true/false and multiple- choice questions, use the course website.

1.   When is it justified to use a group rather than an individual to problem- solve?

2.   Many formats and organizational structures are used in groups. Identify the most common and explain their differences.

3.   An effective problem-solving group uses a structured, rational approach to reach their goals. What are those stages?

4.   Sugar, Tok, Buddy, Sophia, and Taryn are in a problem-solving group. Sugar is the oldest and likes to take charge. Tok makes better grades than the others and lets everyone know he is the smartest. Buddy transferred in from a more prestigious schoo,l and Sophia thinks he is so cute. The two flirt constantly, ignoring the others. Taryn demands perfection and angers easily. What is happening inside this group?

_____ symposium treatment of the emergence stage

_____ parliamentary procedure rules need groupthink

_____ lack of cohesiveness is obviously a problem

_____ brainstorming focus groups never reach decisions

_____ the social interaction calls for a panel discussion

Chapter 10: Thinking Outside the Box: Synthesizing Your Knowledge

These questions are designed to help you develop the big picture by blending what you've learned in this chapter and elsewhere.

1.   Recall an ineffective group you were associated with at some time in the past. What contributed to the group's failure to function up to potential?

2.   Compare the advantages and drawbacks of face-to-face group meetings with those of virtual mediated groups and explain the ideal arrangement.

Chapter 10: Answers to Review Questions

Your answers should include the following:

1,   *Because groups provide the advantage of increased resource availability, better accuracy, and greater commitment, it is recommended to form a group rather than rely on an individual if the job is beyond the capacity of one person, if individual group tasks are interdependent, if more than one decision or solution is possible, and if there is potential for disagreement.*

2.   *A group's structure can shape its ability to come up with high-quality decisions. Breakout groups splinter off from a larger group to address an issue and report back. Problem census allows groups to individualize their problem-solving activity, while soliciting feedback without consideration of personalities. Focus groups consider ideas and submit opinions but do not make a final decision on the matter at hand. Parliamentary procedure rules the conduct of a meeting to keep the discussion on track and to provide the opportunity for everyone in the group to have a voice. Panel discussion formatting encourages conversational participation but does not allow nonmembers to contribute. Symposium structure divides a topic so that each participant contributes to the whole. A forum allows nonmembers to add their opinions to the group's deliberations.*

3.   *The following problem-solving model contains the elements common to most structured approaches essential to effectiveness. Identify the problem. Analyze the problem. Develop creative solutions through brainstorming or the nominal group technique. Evaluate the solutions and implement the plan. Finally, follow up.*

4.   *The members of the problem-solving group will have to address its lack of cohesiveness before it will be possible to achieve the stated goal.*

Chapter 10: Answers to Thinking Outside the Box

1.   *While leadership or lack thereof can complicate the effectiveness of a group, most difficulties arise either because of personalities or improper structure. Wandering off track and allowing distractions to intervene bogs down the effectiveness of a group. If cohesiveness is missing, members become competitive, uninterested, critical of one another, self-centered, and disconnected from the group. Information underload or overload, unequal participation, lack of progress or movement, and pressure to conform could also hamper the ability of the group to function up to potential.*

2.   *Face-to-face groups have immediate and spontaneous interaction.*

Virtual groups have the advantage of offering convenience with regard to time and member availability. Computer-mediated meetings encourage a more balanced participation but eliminate from consideration the nonverbal cues and body language that assist message interpretation in face-to-face settings. There is a record of online communication, whereas incomplete notes or incorrect paraphrases might garble participants memory of a face-to-face meeting. Emotions and attitudes are more easily conveyed face to face. Virtual discussions consume more time, effort, and thought; moreover, they lack the immediacy of face-to-face settings. The personal anonymity of mediated participation often results in more open discussions. While neither form should replace the other completely, a combination that maximizes the strengths of each will improve efficiency and support effectiveness.

CHAPTER 11: PREPARING SPEECHES

SQ3R in Action:

Generate an SQ3R chart for this chapter here:
http://www.teach-nology.com/web_tools/graphic_org/sq3r

Survey

Skim the title, Chapter Highlights, objectives ("You should understand" and "You should be able to"), headings, tables, photos, cartoons, figures, charts, and items in the margin. Glance at the titles of the Critical Thinking Probes and Ethical Challenges. At the end of each chapter, look over the list of Key Terms, Activities, and Resources.

Question

Ask yourself questions. What do you know about these topics from your own life experiences and from other classes? Ask these six questions in each section: who, what, when, where, how, and why.

Read

Take one heading at a time and read to find the answers to the questions you've posed.

Recite

In your own words, say the answer aloud and then write it out.

Review

Review each section and then review the whole chapter. This is a good time to use the activities at the end of each chapter and the activities and the sample exam on the course website. Remember to periodically review the preceding chapters as well.

Chapter 11: Outline

(Italicized words are key terms.)

I.   Public speaking is made easier if the proper tools are used to design and deliver your thoughts effectively.
A.   Choose a topic that is right for you.
B.   Define the *general purpose* of the speech and have a *thesis statement*.
C.   Analyze the speaking situation and gather information.
II.   The fear of public speaking is stronger than the fear of insects, heights, accidents, and even death.
A.   *Debilitative communication apprehension* comes from strong emotions of negative experiences in the past and irrational thinking.
B.   *Facilitative communication apprehension*, which stems from the feeling of not being in control, can be channeled to improve your performance.
C.   Funneling nervous energy into productivity can control fear.
D.   Understanding the difference between rational and *irrational* fears, maintaining an audience-oriented approach with a positive *attitude*, and being prepared are ways to cope with speech anxiety.
III.   The four basic delivery methods for a speech are *extemporaneous, impromptu, manuscript,* and *memorized.*
A.   A smooth natural delivery is the result of extensive practice.
B.   Visual aspects of delivery include appearance, movement, posture, facial expressions, and eye contact.
C.   Auditory aspects of delivery include *volume, rate, pitch, articulation,* and choice of language.

Chapter 11: Summary

The fear of public speaking is ranked over the fear of insects, heights, accidents, and even death. Yet everyone at some time has faced the challenge of giving a speech. There will be more such episodes in the future. By knowing the tools necessary to design and deliver remarks in a clear, interesting, and effective manner you may not grow to love the idea of giving a speech; but you will not dread it as much.

The first task in preparing a speech is to choose the right topic. Choose a topic that interests you. Start there, and then consider whether it is right for the audience and the situation. Once you have found a topic, define the general purpose of your speech. The general purpose should be result oriented, specific, and realistic. Keep focused on the task by stating a thesis that tells the listeners the central idea of your speech. This is usually formulated after you have thought out and researched the topic, but it is presented to the audience as the one idea you want them to remember over everything else.

It is very important to analyze the speaking situation during your preparation. The listener must be considered. Why is the audience present? Do the people want to be there? Reluctant listeners are usually poor listeners. What about the demographic characteristics of your audience? In planning a speech, you should consider cultural diversity, age, gender, group membership, actual number of people present, educational level, and even economic status. What about the attitudes, beliefs, and values of your listeners? Those could be important components for receptivity.

A prepared speaker also focuses on the occasion. What time is the speech being given, and how long should it be? Delivery at six the morning will not be the same as delivery at six at night. Being asked to say a few words is not an invitation to include lengthy reference citations and extensive pontification. All speeches have limits, whether explicitly stated or not. Where is the speech taking place? You prepare differently depending on whether you will be speaking in a coffee shop or on the 50-yard line of a football stadium. What are the audience expectations? If you go to the theatre expecting a comedy, and are presented with a documentary, the surprise will affect your opinion of the show. Your audience approaches listening with the same mind-set.

All speeches benefit from speaker knowledge and expertise in the topic. Do research. Back your words up with outside sources. The Internet is a popular avenue of research; but it is important that your sources have credibility, objectivity, and currency. Consider the practicality of the library. The library catalog, reference works, periodicals, films, tapes, audio files, and databases are rich sources for reinforcing your speech. Interview experts or experienced individuals. Interviews can be conducted face to face, by telephone, via socially mediated communication, or even by using the U.S. Postal Service. If time allows, you could conduct surveys; this will generate results topical to your particular audience. Possessing credible support minimizes the anxiety of thinking you are alone.

Beginning speakers and experienced orators all deal with communication apprehension. A certain amount of nervousness is actually good for a speaker. The pulse rate increases, the mind is more alert, the adrenal energy quickens physical reflexes, and the speaker is emotionally keyed up. These are good things. Facilitative communication apprehension, by preventing you from being too relaxed or lackadaisical, can improve your performance. When the level of anxiety becomes so intense that you cannot think clearly or are impelled to do something, anything, to make the fear go away, you may have a serious problem.

Debilitative communication apprehension inhibits self-expression to the point of physically and emotionally crippling the speaker. People recall earlier negative experiences and trauma and expect the same dire scenarios to be repeated in future situations. Irrational thinking leads one to expect catastrophic failure. Oftentimes the speaker perpetuates a self-fulfilling prophecy by assuming a self-concept of incompetency. Striving for perfection is irrational and unrealistic. Seeking audience approval is a natural desire, but complete acceptance by all is not going to happen. The fallacy of overgeneralization exaggerates one experience to unrealistic proportions. Absolutes such as "always" or "never" take a speaker's internal fears to the fringes of paralyzing insecurity.

There are five strategies that can help you manage debilitative communication apprehension. Use nervousness to your advantage. If your body wants to move, let it; but control and focus the intent. Understand what is rational and irrational. Prepare and obtain knowledge of the speaking situation and avoid fantasies of catastrophe. Maintain a receiver orientation. Concentrate on the audience, not on yourself. Keep a positive attitude. Rather than thinking about what could go wrong, visualize yourself succeeding.

Once you have accepted the charge of presenting a speech, it is time to decide how to deliver the material. Extemporaneous delivery is planned and prepared in advance; then the material is spoken in a direct, spontaneous manner. Impromptu speaking is given on the spur of the moment, off the top of the head, unplanned and unpracticed. Manuscript speeches are written out, comprising a word-for-word text; they are strong on accuracy but weak in spontaneity. Memorized speeches are learned by rote repetition. They lack effectiveness because the presenter concentrates more on recitation and less on relating.

Whichever delivery technique is used, the speaker should consider what is to be seen and heard. Visual aspects of delivery include appearance, movement, posture, facial expressions, and eye contact. Do not allow what the audience is seeing to become a distraction. In addition to choosing the right words, the speaker should be aware of the auditory aspects of delivery, that is, volume, rate, pitch, and articulation. Deletion errors, in which *going, wishing*, and *stopping* turn into *goin', wishin'*, and *stoppin'*, indicate mental laziness that prevents you from completing the sounds. Substitution mistakes occur when you replace part of a word with the incorrect sound so that, for example, *Washington* becomes *War-shington* or *they, them,* and *that* become *dey, dem,* and *dat*. Addition problems add parts to words where they do not belong. *Incentive* grows to *incentative*. *Athlete* expands to *athalete*. *Regardless* turns into *irregardless*. Another articulation challenge is to avoid sacrificing clarity through slurring and overlapping sounds. *Sort of* slides easily into *sorta*. *Kind of* keels over into *kinda*. *Want to* is weakened with *wanna*. How you say what you say sends multiple messages; to speak correctly implies that you are both competent and credible.

Chapter 11: Key Terms

For each of these terms, define the term, give an example, and explain the significance of the term.

1.   addition

2.   articulation

3.   attitude

4.   audience analysis

5.   belief

6.   database

7.   debilitative communication apprehension

8.   deletion

9.   demographics

10.   extemporaneous speech

11.   facilitative communication apprehension

12.   fallacy of approval

13.   fallacy of catastrophic failure

14.   fallacy of overgeneralization

15.   fallacy of perfection

16.   general purpose

17.   impromptu speech

18.   irrational thinking

19.   manuscript speech

20.   memorized speech

21.   purpose statement

22.   rate

23.   slurring

24.   specific purpose

25.   substitution

26.   survey research

27.   thesis statement

28.   value

Chapter 11: Review Questions

These questions are designed to help you understand this chapter's concepts and express your understanding in your own words. For practice with true/false and multiple- choice questions, use the course website.

1.   You know a speech presentation assignment is coming. Getting started is the hard part. What steps should you take?

2.   You are not alone with your fear of public speaking. What are the two types of speech anxiety, and how can you manage them?

3.   Planning and preparing a speech sets the scene for how you deliver the speech. Identify your delivery choices, listing their advantages and disadvantages.

4.   You have two choices for an informative speech in your British lit class. You know one topic is the professor's favorite author. The other possibility has not been mentioned in class at all this semester, but you think it is fascinating. Which topic do you choose?

        _____ get in the teacher's good graces and take the author

        _____ if the other has not been discussed, it must not be good

        _____ the professor is smarter than you, so the author known to be favored is the right choice

_____ with research, the second choice could be interesting to everyone

_____ authors are easier to research, so take that route

Chapter 11: Thinking Outside the Box: Synthesizing Your Knowledge

These questions are designed to help you develop the big picture by blending what you've learned in this chapter and elsewhere.

1.   Out of the blue, you are asked to speak next week on the topic of checkers as a learning tool in elementary school. The person extending the request wants to know if you have any questions. Well?

2.   As you prepare for delivery of a speech, practice is essential. How should you practice, and what two guidelines should you consider in getting your message across to the audience? Give specifics.

Chapter 11: Answers to Review Questions

Your answers should include the following:

1.   *Choose your topic, determine your purpose, and find information. Use a variety of sources to increase your credibility. Take the audience into consideration. Why are they there? Do they want to be present? Consider the demographics of the audience. Audience members' feelings about you, your topic, and your intentions will flavor their reception. It is beneficial to research your listeners. Prepare for the occasion by knowing the time allotted for the speech as well as when and where it is being presented.*

2.   *Facilitative communication apprehension is a normal feeling experienced by all. Being comfortable with the preparation of the speech, and your knowledge of the occasion, will allow you to focus the nervousness to your advantage. This keeps you alert and on your toes. When your quickening pulse increases the flow of blood to the brain, that means more oxygen to your brain, which gives you faster thought processes, clearer vision, and better reflexes. Directed and controlled, nervousness can add zest and vigor to your presentation. When anxiety reaches the stage of irrational fears, however, it becomes debilitative communication apprehension. Recalling past negative experiences and projecting them to the future is illogical, but people do it frequently. Being*

consumed with irrational thoughts that include worries over catastrophic failure, inability to attain perfection, audience disapproval, and overgeneralizations can cause a speaker to either freeze or flee. Think before you speak and accept reality. You are not perfect. Neither is anyone else. What is important is the message the listeners get. Think positive thoughts and, instead of being your worst critic and constantly finding fault, visualize success. .

3. *Extemporaneous delivery is planned and prepared in advance and then delivered in a direct, spontaneous manner. Because your tone is conversational, the listeners feel you are communicating with them and not at them. Impromptu speeches are delivered without advance planning, that is, at the spur of the moment, off the top of the head. The immediacy of the remarks adds freshness and reflects sincere emotions; but the requirement for spontaneous delivery hampers coherent organization. Manuscript speeches require time to prepare. Written out and read word for word, they tend to be the most accurate, but variety in vocal delivery often is stilted because of lack of spontaneity. Memorized delivery is learned from repeated rehearsals and is the most difficult to carry off with any sense of realism.*

4. *One of the first rules in getting started on a speech is to choose a topic that interests you. If you find a subject fascinating, you can then research supporting material to motivate the listeners to find it interesting, too.*

Chapter 11: Answers to Thinking Outside the Box

1. *In no particular order of importance, you want the following questions answered. To whom am I talking? What will the audience be like in terms of cultural diversity, age, gender, group membership, number of people, education level, maybe even economic status and year in school or major subject? Does the audience want to be there, and what are they expecting? What are their attitudes, beliefs, and values regarding checkers and elementary education? How long am I supposed to talk? When is the speech? Where? What type speech is expected? Should it be informative or persuasive? Is someone speaking before me or after me? You may have follow-up questions after you have the answers to your first set, but it will be to your advantage if the initial questions are answered as soon as possible.*

2. *First, present the speech to yourself. Talk through the speech from beginning to middle to end. Use your support and visual aids during*

rehearsal. If possible, record your speech so you can watch and hear yourself. Critique but do not criticize. Rework, rewrite, and rehearse again. Get a volunteer, friend, or family member to be your focus group. Try the speech out on this small audience. Solicit constructive feedback. Rehearse again. If possible, walk through the presentation with sound, movement, and all support in the location of the finished product. Constantly hone the visual aspects of delivery, paying attention to movement, appearance, posture, facial expressions, gestures, and eye contact. Evaluate your choice of language, and practice controlling the auditory aspects of delivery. Recognize and use appropriate volume, rate, pitch, and articulation.

CHAPTER 12: ORGANIZATION AND SUPPORT

SQ3R in Action:

Generate an SQ3R chart for this chapter here:
        http://www.teach-nology.com/web_tools/graphic_org/sq3r

Survey

Skim the title, Chapter Highlights, objectives ("You should understand" and
"You should be able to"), headings, tables, photos, cartoons, figures, charts, and items in the margin. Glance at the titles of the Critical Thinking Probes and Ethical Challenges. At the end of each chapter, look over the list of Key Terms, Activities, and Resources.

Question

Ask yourself questions. What do you know about these topics from your own life experiences and from other classes? Ask these six questions in each section: who, what, when, where, how, and why.

Read

Take one heading at a time and read to find the answers to the questions you've posed.

Recite

In your own words, say the answer aloud and then write it out.

Review

Review each section and then review the whole chapter. This is a good time to use the activities at the end of each chapter and the activities and the sample exam on the course website. Remember to periodically review the

preceding chapters as well.

Chapter 12: Outline

(Italicized words are key terms.)

I. A good speech is like a good building. It requires a plan, a blueprint.
    A. *Working outlines*, formal outlines, or speaking notes solidify ideas and structurally reinforce the impact of the content.
    B. There should be a logical *basic speech structure* that makes use of *time patterns*, *space patterns*, *topic patterns*, *problem–solution patterns*, or *cause–effect patterns*.
    C. *Transitions* keep your message moving forward and show the relation of one part of the speech to the next.
II. How you start and how you finish are vital for the effectiveness of your speech.
    A. The *introduction* should capture attention, preview main points, set the mood and tone of the speech, and demonstrate the importance of your topic.
    B. The *conclusion* should restate the thesis, review main points, and provide a memorable ending.
    C. Avoid a rambling uncertain beginning and a finale that ends abruptly, rambles on, introduces main points, or apologizes for weaknesses.
III. Organize the main points in a clear, logical manner that is reinforced with supporting material.
    A. Supporting material clarifies, helps make interesting, makes memorable, and proves.
    B. Available resources include but are not limited to definitions, *examples*, *statistics*, *analogies*, comparisons and contrasts, *anecdotes*, quotations, and *testimony* through either *narration* or *citation*.

Chapter 12: Summary

A good speech is like a good building. Both grow from a careful plan. The clear, repetitive nature of the basic structure of a speech reduces the potential for memory loss. A working outline maps out the speech. Since it is for your eyes only, it can be in rough-draft form, available for revisions and polish as you go along. A formal outline has a consistent format and set of symbols to identify the structure of ideas. It is a simplified form of your presentation and can be displayed as a visual aid or a handout. Speaking notes list information in brief key-word fashion, providing just enough to jog your memory.

There should be a logical order to the outline or speaking notes. Time patterns arrange details according to chronological order. Space patterns are arranged according to area. Topic patterns base the arrangement on types or categories. Problem–solution patterns are used primarily in persuasive speeches: they describe a wrong and propose a solution. Cause–effect patterns discuss something that happened and then discuss the effects of the event.

Transitions keep your message moving forward. Transitions should refer to the preceding point and lead to the upcoming point. Maybe the transition will be an internal review, restating earlier points, or a preview looking ahead. Transitions connect the relationship of the introduction to the body, of main points to subpoints, and of body to conclusion.

Listeners form their impression of a speaker early; so use the beginning of your speech to capture attention, preview the main points, set the mood and tone of the speech, and demonstrate the importance of the topic. Several choices are possible in capturing the attention of the audience. You could refer to the audience, refer to the occasion, refer to the relationship between audience and subject, refer to something familiar, cite a startling point, ask a question, tell an anecdote, use a quote, or tell a joke. Whichever device is selected should also set the stage fr the main points and thesis of the presentation. How the speaker starts is what tells the audience how to listen. The speaker sets the mood and tone of the speech by immediately communicating confidence, comfort, and competence. The message or topic must relate to the audience directly. If your audience is caused to see the importance of the topic and to realize how it affects them, the people will listen more attentively.

A strong, definite, solid conclusion can enhance or minimize the impact of your speech. The conclusion has three essential functions: to restate the thesis, to review your main points, and to provide a memorable final remark. You can make your final remark most effective by avoiding the following mistakes: ending abruptly, rambling on and on and on and on and on and on, introducing points that should have been covered in the body of the speech, and apologizing for weaknesses and mistakes.

It is important to organize ideas clearly and logically; backing up and proving your ideas and opinions, however, is the role of supporting material. Supporting material clarifies, adds to interest, makes memorable, and proves. These functions can be accomplished by means of definitions, examples, statistics, analogies, comparisons and contrasts, anecdotes, quotations, and testimony. Narrative supporting material is presented in the form of telling a story. Narration implies relating and connectivity. Citation states the facts in a shorter more precise manner. Citation is clear and direct. Both narration and citation have presentation advantages, depending on the delivery technique of the speaker.

Chapter 12: Key Terms

For each of these terms, define the term, give an example, and explain the significance of the term.

a. analogy

b. anecdote

c. basic speech structure

d. cause–effect pattern

e. citation

f. climax pattern

g. conclusion

h. example

i. hypothetical example

j. introduction (of a speech)

k. narration

l. problem–solution pattern

m. space pattern

n. statistic

o. testimony

p. time pattern

q. topic pattern

r. transition

s. working outline

Chapter 12: Review Questions

These questions are designed to help you understand this chapter's concepts and express your understanding in your own words. For practice with true/false and multiple- choice questions, use the course website.

1.   Clear organization is important for refining ideas and building a framework for your message. You have a choice of three structures to use. Cite them and explain the advantages of each.

2.   There should be a logical order to your points. What organizing patterns are available for you to best develop your thesis?

3.   What are the functions of a speech introduction? Why are they important?

4.   Identify the three essential roles of the conclusion of a speech.

5.   You and another were assigned basically the same speech topic. The other person spoke first, and while the ideas were clearly and logically expressed, the class seemed bored. When your turn came you used visual aids, clarified definitions, did a demonstration, and explained how the material related to the audience. The audience responded energetically. Why did your speech 'work' and not your classmate's?

_____ the person going first is always at a disadvantage

_____ you used supporting material to flesh out the main points

_____ hearing the same material twice wakes an audience up

_____ everyone knows logic is boring

_____ going second meant it was closer to the end of class

Chapter 12: Thinking Outside the Box: Synthesizing Your Knowledge

These questions are designed to help you develop the big picture by blending what you've learned in this chapter and elsewhere.

1.   Your speech topic is "The fire ant." It is important that you capture the attention of the audience immediately. What are your options?

Cite examples.

2.　　"The fire ant" speech obviously needs supporting material. What tools do you have at your disposal to clarify, add interest, make memorable, and prove?

Chapter 12: Answers to Review Questions

Your answers should include the following:

1.　*The three structures to use for refining ideas and building the framework for your message are a working outline, a formal outline, and speaking notes. A working outline is for your eyes only and will be a rough-draft tool to help you refine and hone the presentation. It might go through several revisions as you solidify your ideas; but it is a consistent guide to follow in staying on task to achieve your general purpose. A formal outline uses a consistent structure. It uses standard symbols, a standard format, set rules of division, and parallel wording of outline construction. It could be a visual aid or a handout. Another person should be able to understand the basics of your speech by reading the formal outline. Speaking notes are for your use only. By means of key words or phrases, the speaking notes jog your memory without resorting to the stilted, nonspontaneous, manuscript format of word-for-word delivery.*

2.　*An outline should impart a logical order to your points. Arrangement of time patterns, or chronological order, is one of the most commonly used forms. Space patterns organize according to area, whereas topic patterns use categories. Problem–solution patterns describe what is wrong and then propose a way to make things better. Cause–effect patterns discuss what happened, then discuss the effects that were produced.*

3.　*A speech introduction serves to capture the audience's attention, preview the main points, set the mood and tone of the speech, and demonstrate the importance of the topic. The introduction is vitally important because listeners form their opinions of a speaker early. Stimulating interest and motivating the audience to want to listen is the major function of the introduction.*

4.　*Since audience members remember what they hear last, the conclusion is especially important. The conclusion has three major functions: to restate the thesis, to review main points, and to provide a memorable final remark. Mistakes that should be avoided in a conclusion include ending abruptly, and rambling on and on and on without a definite end. Two other mistakes to avoid are introducing new points after you have signaled that you are wrapping up and apologizing for weaknesses and presentation errors.*

5.   *Your speech had the attention of the audience and was more effective than the other one because you used supporting material to flesh out the main points.*

Chapter 12: Answers to Thinking Outside the Box

1.   *The options for capturing the attention of the audience in your introduction are varied and immediate. With "The fire ant" as the topic, one choice would be to refer to the audience: "This nice classroom would not be so quiet if three, four, or five of you were suddenly bitten by fire ants." Referring to the occasion alludes to an event: "Today is Stay Away from Fire Ants Day. If you do not, you will have a painful reminder of how these creatures got their name. Fire ant." Referring to the relationship between audience and subject can be an attention-getter: "We all know how awful it is to have your summer day ruined by a bite from a fire ant." Referring to something familiar is another way to cause your audience to pay attention: "See that innocent-looking mound of dirt? Stay away from it. Stay far away from it." A startling statement of fact or opinion also can cause the audience to sit up and listen: "One bite from a fire ant can kill a grown man." Or you could start your speech by asking a question: "Who here has not been bitten by a fire ant?" A rhetorical question can cause the audience to think: "Ever wonder how a creature as small as a fire ant can cause so much pain?" Anecdotes show the human side of the speaker: "My first encounter with the dreaded fire ant was as a newlywed. What happened was. . . ." Quotations work: "Prominent lawn and garden expert Neil Sperry once called the fire ant the most evil creature in America." Maybe you could start your speech with a joke: "You do know the popular dance move 'The Stomp' was invented because of fire ants in the house?"*

2.   *With research and effort, the speech about "The fire ant" could be very effective, especially if you use a combination of definitions, examples, statistics, analogies, comparisons and contrasts, anecdotes, quotations, and testimony. Most forms of support can be presented by either narration or citation. Narration involves telling a story with your information. Examples, analogies, anecdotes, even comparing and contrasting supporting material, fit*

the narration method. Citations are shorter and more precise. Definitions, statistics, quotations, and testimony work well as citations. However, the speaker's comfort and personality should always be the prime factor in deciding whether to express and use narrations or citations.

CHAPTER 13: INFORMATIVE SPEAKING

SQ3R in Action:

Generate an SQ3R chart for this chapter here:
http://www.teach-nology.com/web_tools/graphic_org/sq3r

Survey

Skim the title, Chapter Highlights, objectives ("You should understand" and "You should be able to"), headings, tables, photos, cartoons, figures, charts, and items in the margin. Glance at the titles of the Critical Thinking Probes and Ethical Challenges. At the end of each chapter, look over the list of Key Terms, Activities, and Resources.

Question

Ask yourself questions. What do you know about these topics from your own life experiences and from other classes? Ask these six questions in each section: who, what, when, where, how, and why.

Read

Take one heading at a time and read to find the answers to the questions you've posed.

Recite

In your own words, say the answer aloud and then write it out.

Review

Review each section and then review the whole chapter. This is a good time to use the activities at the end of each chapter and the activities and the sample exam on the course website. Remember to periodically review the preceding chapters as well.

Chapter 13: Outline

(Italicized words are key terms.)

I.   Today's informative speaker has the responsibility of taking *information overload*, or *information anxiety*, and turning it into *knowledge understanding*.
  - A.   Informative speeches are generally categorized according to content or purpose.
  - B.   Speeches about objects, processes, events, and concepts are content driven.
  - C.   Speeches with *descriptions*, *explanations*, and *instructions* are purpose driven.
  - D.   Unlike a persuasive speech, an informative speech should not be controversial, nor should its intent be to change audience attitudes.

II.   To help an audience understand, informative speakers should apply specific techniques.
  - A.   Informative speeches should create *information hunger*, make it easy to listen, use clear and simple language, define a specific informative purpose, and use clear organization and structure.
  - B.   Informative speeches should use supporting material effectively, emphasize important points, and generate *audience involvement* through *audience participation*.

III.   *Visual aids* are especially important in informative speeches.
  - A.   Visual aids might include objects, *models*, *diagrams*, *word* and *number charts*, *pie charts*, *bar* and *column charts*, or *line charts*.
  - B.   Other visual aids possible are chalkboards, whiteboards, polymer marking surfaces, flip pads, poster board, handouts, projectors, or mediated devices such slide shows, PowerPoint, websites, DVDs, CDs, and film.
  - C.   No matter what visual aid you choose, always consider simplicity, size, attractiveness, appropriateness, and reliability.

Chapter 13: Summary

Maybe we do live in what is called the "information age"; but the truth is, most of us suffers from information overload leading to information anxiety. We have psychological stress from the challenges of sorting gossip from fact, truth from supposition, information from persuasion. Because of this, the informative speaker's responsibility is to provide not just information but information knowledge.

Informative speeches are categorized according to type: content or purpose. A content-oriented speech can be about objects, processes, events, or concepts. They deal with tangible or specific results. An informative speech of the content type deals with what happened, what might happen, beliefs, theories, ideas and principles. Purpose-driven informative speeches use description, explanations, and instructions to create a word picture of the essentials. A speech to teach, show, or answer the question *why* is considered an informative speech with a purpose. Informative speeches differ from persuasive speeches because the former tend to be noncontroversial and because the speaker does not intend to change audience attitudes.

To help the audience understand, informative speeches should create information hunger, which gives the listeners a reason to want to hear more. Speakers should make it easy to listen by limiting the amount of information provided to a concise, controllable amount and by using the familiar to increase understanding of the unfamiliar. Clear, simple language is preferred. The speaker should define a specific informative purpose with a clear organization and structure. Supporting material must be effective, serving to emphasize important points. Audience involvement increases acquisition of knowledge. This occurs through personalization, audience participation, volunteers, and a question-and-answer period.

Visual aids are extremely useful in informative speeches because they illustrate and support ideas. The most commonly used visual aids are objects and models, diagrams, word and number charts, pie charts, bar and column charts, and line charts. Media devices complement and enhance traditional aids. Chalkboards, whiteboards, polymer marking surfaces, flip charts, poster board, handouts, projectors, and electronic mediated applications such as audiovisual appliances, films, PowerPoint, slides, DVDs, CDs, websites, and recording devices all can be used to advantage with today's audiences.

Visual aids should be utilized only if they are simple enough to offer clarification instead of leading to confusion. Size matters. The audience should not have to work to see your graphics or printed text. Attractiveness earns interest points. Appropriateness and reliability emphasize credibility. Talk to your audience, not to your visuals. The visual aid assists and does not overwhelm. It complements without dominating. Practice with your visual aid ahead of time. Do not let the first time your audience sees it be the first time you see it. You control the visual aid, not the other way around.

Chapter 13: Key Terms

For each of these terms, define the term, give an example, and explain the significance of the term.

1.   audience involvement

2.   audience participation

3.   bar chart

4.   column chart

5.   description

6.   diagram

7.   explanations

8.   information anxiety

9.   information hunger

10. information overload

11. informative purpose statement

12. instructions

13. knowledge

14. line chart

15. model

16. number chart

17. pie chart

18. signpost

19. visual aids

20. word chart

Chapter 13: Review Questions

These questions are designed to help you understand this chapter's concepts and express your understanding in your own words. For practice with true/false and multiple- choice questions, use the course website.

1.   You are asked to present an informative speech but are not sure whether it should be driven by content or by purpose. What is the difference, and why does it matter?

2.   To avoid a stereotypically dry, dull documentary-style delivery in your informative speech, you want to create information hunger. What is that, and how can it be achieved?

3.   What are the benefits of including visual aids in an informative speech?

4   A classmate approaches you with a dilemma. She has to present an   informative speech on convection/microwave ovens and needs help in   choosing visual aids. You recommend that she

_____ tell about the first time she cooked popcorn in a microwave

_____ cook enough popcorn for everyone in the class and pass it out

_____ demonstrate how a convection/microwave oven works

_____ ask for everyone who does not own a microwave to raise their hand

_____ make copies of the instruction manual and pass them around

Chapter 13: Thinking Outside the Box: Synthesizing Your Knowledge

These questions are designed to help you develop the big picture by blending what you've learned in this chapter and elsewhere.

1. In this age of information, you are constantly bombarded with pop-ups on your monitor and by billboards, ads in magazines, and commercials

on radio and television. Over the course of one day, keep track of this information overload and decide if what you are receiving is informative or persuasive. How can you tell? Explain your answer.

2. You have been a member of the audience for an informative speech somewhere, some time in the past. Think back and evaluate the effectiveness of the visual aids used according to the five guidelines stipulated in Chapter 13.

Chapter 13: Answers to Review Questions

Your answers should include the following:

1.   *To order to turn information into knowledge, the premise of the speech, the spine, the gist, the specific informative purpose, focuses on the material. Content-driven informative speeches sometimes use objects as the focal point. The speech is about the object. Some presentations construct the speech around the attempt to ensure that the listener understands the process, or series of actions leading to a specific result. A speech relating to events, those in the past or those upcoming, is driven by content. With speeches touching on beliefs, ideas, principles, and concepts, the content is the message. But if the purpose of the speech is to describe, explain, or instruct, then you must alter the structure slightly. Purpose-driven informative speeches are more straightforward. Creating "word pictures" and dealing with the question of "why" and logical step-by-step instructions can also include demonstration. These two types of informative speech are not mutually exclusive. They do often overlap, but the speaker should always organize according to a predetermined plan of what is to be accomplished by the end of the speech.*

2.   *Information hunger is defined as the reason for your audience members to want to listen to and learn from your speech. In addition to addressing either physical, identity, social, or practical needs, the speaker must relate to the listener so that a mutual connection is created. The speaker should make it easy to listen. Do not ask the listener to work. Limit the amount of information to avoid potential information anxiety. Use familiar information as a foundation to take the listener into unfamiliar territory. Keep things simple at first, then build in more complexity. Use clear, simple language. Your sentences should be direct and short. Depending on your audience and how much they already know about your topic, you can expand and enlarge your vocabulary, but only if you*

always strive for listener comprehension. A clear, definite, specific informative purpose keeps you and the audience on task. An organizational structure with specifically delineated components assists the audience in listening, provided important points are supported with effective emphasis. Getting the audience involved through personalizing the speech, inviting the audience to participate, asking for volunteers, and announcing a question-and-answer period are means of giving the audience a reason to continue listening.

3. *Visual aids illustrate and support ideas. Visual aids are a method of clarification, enabling the listener to see the process as well as hear it. They can offer proof, which in turn enhances the speaker's credibility and competence. Visual aids are memory enhancement devices that impact the brain with deeper and longer lasting retention. Visual aids increase interest. They highlight certain words to combine sight with sound for the listener. Visual aids can actually take words out of the mouth of the speaker by allowing the listeners to think and absorb on their own. Visual aids enhance all speeches, but they are especially important in informative speeches.*

4. *While anecdotes can be used to get the attention of the audience at the beginning of a speech, they are not visual aids. Most students like popcorn, but the distraction of an entire class munching could take away from the presentation. Pointing out economic differences in the audience is not a good way to establish a connection, nor is it a visual aid in line with the specific informative purpose. Handouts encourage audience participation; but does your friend want audience members reading the material in hand and ignoring the speaker in front of them? So the correct answer is: demonstrating in class how a convection/microwave works would underline and support the speech most effectively.*

Chapter 13: Answers to Thinking Outside the Box

1. *Observations taken over even a short period reveal that the majority of material flooding our senses via media is persuasive in nature. How can you tell? While most persuasive presentations use information as a tool; the major differences between persuasive and informative speeches lie in the answers to two questions: categories. First, is it controversial? Second, is change desired? It is very difficult to disagree with facts. That is what an informative speech contains. Information knowledge is not controversial, and*

those who attempt to make it so are subverting an informative message into a persuasive one to engender conflict. That is not the purpose of an informative speech. The second criterion addresses whether the information is being delivered with the intent to change audience attitudes. Commercials on radio and television, billboards, computer pop-ups, and ads in magazines are there to sell products. The intent is to make the audience feel differently, to choose, to select, to agree, and to take action because of that feeling. Showing the class how a convection/microwave oven works is informative. Advocating one particular brand over another or finding fault with the safety standards of convection/microwaves in comparison to gas cookstoves turns the delivery into persuasion.

2. *Speech presentations succeed or fail depending on the interest and involvement of the audience. Making the audience work is very likely to produce failure. Visual aids should enhance, highlight, underline, clarify, prove, add to interest, and strengthen memory. This is best done by keeping things simple. Use key words and phrases, not complete sentences. Go bare bones and flesh out the aids with your spoken words. Be sure the visuals are large enough to be seen by all. The visuals should be eye-catching and attractive. Neatness counts. Use only appropriate visuals that pertain to the main points. Visuals must be reliable. There will be questions about the credibility of a speaker who does not demonstrate competence and mastery of the technology and challenges of displaying visual aids.*

CHAPTER 14: PERSUASIVE SPEAKING

SQ3R in Action:

Generate an SQ3R chart for this chapter here:
http://www.teach-nology.com/web_tools/graphic_org/sq3r

Survey

Skim the title, Chapter Highlights, objectives ("You should understand" and "You should be able to"), headings, tables, photos, cartoons, figures, charts, and items in the margin. Glance at the titles of the Critical Thinking Probes and Ethical Challenges. At the end of each chapter, look over the list of Key Terms, Activities, and Resources.

Question

Ask yourself questions. What do you know about these topics from your own life experiences and from other classes? Ask these six questions in each section: who, what, when, where, how, and why.

Read

Take one heading at a time and read to find the answers to the questions you've posed.

Recite

In your own words, say the answer aloud and then write it out.

Review

Review each section and then review the whole chapter. This is a good time to use the activities at the end of each chapter and the activities and the sample exam on the course website. Remember to periodically review the preceding chapters as well.

Chapter 14: Outline

(Italicized words are key terms.)

I.   *Persuasion* is the process of motivating someone, through communication, to change a particular belief, attitude, or behavior.
    A.   Implicit in the definition of persuasion is the principle that coerciveness is unethical.
    B.   Persuasion usually occurs in increments; normally results are neither instant nor dramatic.
    C.   To be effective, persuasion must be interactive.
    D.   Ethical persuasion avoids coercion and communicates in the best interest of the audience without the use of false or misleading information.

II.   To present persuasive topics, one must keep in mind the proposed change, focusing on subject, results, and method of achieving those results.
    A.   *Proposition of fact* messages ask listeners to choose between two or more sides.
    B.   *Proposition of value* speeches explore the worth of an idea, person, or object.
    C.   *Proposition of policy* persuasions recommend a specific course of action.
    D.   Whether the speaker attempts to persuade through *convincing* or by stimulating a result to *actuate* the desired outcome depends on the speaker's appreciation of the listener's receptivity to a *direct* or *indirect* approach.

III.   To create an effective persuasive speech, the speaker must structure a message with strong reason-giving justification.
    A.   A clear and definite persuasive purpose must be obvious.
    B.   The message must be structured carefully with the desired outcome in mind.
    C.   Solid evidence is essential.
    D.   A speaker should always avoid logical fallacies. These errors in logic will ruin a persuasive argument and eliminate any rapport the speaker might have had with the listener.

IV.   Advance knowledge of the audience and anticipated responses gives the speaker the opportunity to adapt to the audience.
    A.   The speaker has to establish common ground with the audience.
    B.   Always organize the speech according to the expected response.
    C.   Be prepared to neutralize potential hostility. Given the general reluctance to change, it is essential for the speaker to anticipate disagreement.

V.   The strongest support a persuasive speaker possesses is *credibility*.
    A.   Perception in the minds of listeners determines a speaker's believability.
    B.   Credibility has the three components of competence, character, and charisma.

Chapter 14: Summary

Persuasion is the process of motivating someone, through communication, to change a particular belief, attitude, or behavior. There are several paths to the achievement of persuasion, and one component can be characterized as the unethical use of coercion. Coercion is forced, unwilling change, whereas ethical persuasion has the more lasting effect of getting the listener to want to think or act differently. Persuasion is usually incremental; that is, change is neither instant nor dramatic. Realistically, listeners begin with a preexisting opinion called their anchor and gradually move along the latitude of rejection to latitude of noncommitment and then to the latitude of acceptance. Because persuasion is interactive, it is undertaken with the audience, as opposed to being imposed on others. Ethical persuasion plays a necessary role in everyone's life. Persuasive communication is ethical if it is in the best interest of the audience and does not depend on false or misleading information.

In considering the subjects of focus, the desired results, and the methods used to achieve those results, a speaker can choose from among different types of persuasion. The proposition of facts message presents two or more sides, asking listeners to choose the truth for themselves. Proposition of value persuasions explore the worth of an idea, person, or object. Propositions of policy go one step beyond the question of fact or value and recommend a specific course of action. The desired outcome of delivery of the persuasive message is either to persuade the audience to change, and maybe to reinforce and strengthen current positions, or to move the members to take action. In a direct approach, usually used before a friendly audience, a speaker makes the desired outcome obvious. The indirect approach, de-emphasizing the desired outcome in anticipation of reluctance or hostility from the audience, calls for the use of more information to ease into the areas listeners find uncomfortable or disagreeable.

Often persuasion is termed a "reason-giving discourse." The goal is to give the listeners a justifiable reason to change. This can be achieved only through an effective, well-constructed persuasive message. There must be a persuasive purpose that is clear and definite. The message should be structured with a view to defining a situation as one that needs changing and describing a solution that incorporates the change you are advocating. The speaker should describe the nature of the problem and its effect on the audience. The speaker should also describe the proposed solution. Why will the solution work? What advantages would result from accepting the solution? The speaker should be clear in describing the desired audience response. What can the audience do to implement the solution; and what are the rewards of the desired response? Monroe's Motivated Sequence breaks down the persuasive steps into an attention step and a need step; and the solution is broken down into a satisfaction step, a visualization step, and an action step. Solid evidence is essential. The speaker needs supporting material that is credible, unbiased, and current.

A persuasive speaker is effective only if the audience accepts the justification for change as ethical and logical. Too often, persuasive speakers commit errors in logic, referred to as logical fallacies, ruining credibility. The *ad hominem* fallacy attacks the person instead of the argument. This makes the issue the messenger rather than the message. *Reductio ad absurdum* fallacies unfairly attack an argument by extending it to laughable extremes, mocking and ridiculing the argument without offering verifiable proof. The either-or fallacy uses ultimatums and the misconception that only two choices exist—and since one is obviously inferior, the other must be accepted. *Post hoc, ergo propter hoc* fallacies assume a false cause as logical reasoning, suggesting that one event caused another because they occurred sequentially. The fallacious *argumentum ad verecundiam* attempts to prove a point by means of the testimony of well-known but unqualified sources. This appeal to authority assumes that celebrity means credibility, and such is seldom the case. Another fallacy, known as the *argumentum ad populum*, makes the case that because a decision is popular and favored by a majority, it is the correct one. This is not always true; yet some use the bandwagon effect created by this fallacy to signal that mass appeal means meritorious appeal. Sincere listeners do not follow the crowd; they instead consider the facts and make up their minds accordingly, as individuals.

Audience analysis is important for a persuasive speaker because it is helpful to stress similarities between yourself and your audience members. Establishing a common ground shows that despite differences, there are areas of understanding and respect. A prepared persuasive speech anticipates and is organized according to the expected response of the listeners. It is much easier to get an audience to agree with you if the members have already accepted one of your early points. This willingness to show that you understand their point of view enables you to neutralize potential hostility when your call for change is stated.

The ideas of many speakers are rejected before their speech gets under way because of a perceived lack of credibility. The believability of the speaker can grow or wane during the course of the speech; it represents a series of judgment calls on the part of the audience members. Credibility is made up of the "three Cs" of competence, character, and charisma. The speaker's expertise on the subject, competence, includes experience in addition to a well-prepared, well-substantiated presentation. Character elements of trust include the two ingredients of honesty and impartiality. While difficult to define specifically, charisma refers to the audience's perception of enthusiasm and likability. Credibility combined with a careful consideration of audience adaptation, persuasive structure, and persuasive purpose, will enable you to formulate the most effective call for change.

Chapter 14: Key Terms

For each of these terms, define the term, give an example, and explain the significance of the term.

1. actuate

2. ad hominem fallacy

3. anchor

4. argumentum ad populum fallacy

5. argumentum ad verecundiam fallacy

6. convincing

7. credibility

8. direct persuasion

9. either-or fallacy

10. emotional evidence

11. ethical persuasion

12. evidence

13. fallacy

14. indirect persuasion

15. latitude of acceptance

16. latitude of noncommitment

17.   latitude of rejection

18.   motivated sequence

19.   persuasion

20.   post hoc, ergo propter hoc fallacy

21.   proposition of fact

22.   proposition of policy

23.   proposition of value

24.   reductio ad absurdum fallacy

25.   social judgment theory

26.   target audience

Chapter 14: Review Questions

These questions are designed to help you understand this chapter's concepts and express your understanding in your own words. For practice with true/false and multiple- choice questions, use the course website.

1.   Define persuasion and identify its characteristics.

2.   Why is it important for a persuasive speaker to select a desired outcome and directness of approach? Explain your answer.

3.   A clear, specific, attainable movement by the audience depends on the structure and organization of the persuasive speech. Describe a basic persuasive speech model.

4.   A speaker should avoid logical fallacies. What are the most common ones?

5.   You open your persuasive speech with an apology because the visual aids are not adequate. You reveal that you have a vested interest in the decision of the audience, perhaps because it could mean a payroll bonus for you. You grow tired of frequent questions during the speech, and your delivery loses steam before the conclusion. Later you are told that your opinions were not worth consideration. What happened?

_____ a persuasive speech is hampered without good visual aids and so you did not stand a chance

_____ too many people had an anchor position of reluctance to change, and so their latitude of rejection defeated you

_____ you should not have allowed questions during the content of the speech as that gives dissenters too much attention

_____ you were perceived as incompetent, without character, and lacking charisma

_____ you did not get your payroll bonus, which isn't fair because your opinions do have merit

Chapter 14: Thinking Outside the Box: Synthesizing Your Knowledge

These questions are designed to help you develop the big picture by blending what you've learned in this chapter and elsewhere.

1.   Why are persuasive speeches so difficult? You know you are right in your assertion, yet others do not feel or think the same way. What can you do, before the time comes to speak up, to improve your chances for acceptance?

2.   Observe and pay attention to one hour of network television and note the barrage of persuasive presentations in that short period. Which ones used the direct approach and which the indirect? Give specifics. Why did you find some more effective than others? Explain your answer.

Chapter 14: Answers to Review Questions

Your answers should include the following:

1.   *Persuasion is the process of motivating someone, through communication, to change a particular belief, attitude, or behavior. It should not be coercive; rather, it should progress incrementally, recognizing the social judgment theory (that is, that your audience will compare your contentions to the opinions they already hold); and it should be designed so that the persuasion is done with the audience, not to them. Persuasion can and should be ethical.*

2.   *The structure and preparation of a persuasive speech hinges on the speaker's desired outcome. The speaker should know as much as possible about the audience and, depending on whether the goal is to convince, to sway, or to motivate the audience, the speaker should aim the delivery accordingly. Knowledge of the audience will assist the speaker in determining degree of urgency— for example, whether the task is to reinforce or strengthen current attitudes. When a speaker sets out to actuate an audience, a specific behavior is desired. You can ask for adoption or discontinuance. You may want people to undertake a new behavior or stop an old one. Depending on the response expected from the audience, the desired outcome can be presented either directly—to a friendly or neutral audience—or indirectly—to a reluctant or hostile audience.*

3.   *To order to create a clear and effective persuasive speech, your thoughts must be logical and your argument well structured. Set a clear persuasive purpose, establishing the message with clarity and presenting it progressively. Describe the problem; tell how it affects your audience; describe the preferred solution; then tell how it will work and state what advantages the audience can expect if they accept your proposition. Tell the audience what you want from them and what they can do. Cite direct rewards and benefits. Always use credible solid evidence and avoid logical fallacies. Monroe's Motivated Sequence organizes the persuasive contention into five steps: attention, need, satisfaction, visualization, and action.*

4.   *The most common logical fallacies are attack on the person (ad hominem), reduction to the absurd (reductio ad absurdum), either-or, false cause (post hoc, ergo propter hoc), appeal to authority (argumentum ad verecundiam), and bandwagon appeal (argumentum ad populum)*

5.   *Every indicator, from the start of the presentation through the content portion and continued to the conclusion, shows that you lost credibility. The audience perceived you as incompetent, without character, and lacking charisma.*

Chapter 14: Answers to Thinking Outside the Box

1. *One reason for the difficulty of making an effective persuasive speech is that the feeling you are right and others are wrong starts often starts the speaker off on an uncomfortable sometimes arrogant path. The issue is not always as obvious as a certain right and a definite wrong. What about the attitudes, beliefs, values, and opinions of the audience? Could it be that they think they are right and you are wrong? It is important to know as much as possible about your audience. It helps reception if you establish as many similarities as possible between yourself and the members of your audience. Even strenuous advocates of diametrically opposite convictions share a common ground that must be identified if you are seeking resolution. The speaker should always organize the presentation, including the desired outcome, according to the expected response. To neutralize potential hostility, you must show your respectful understanding of the point of view of the audience and, at the same time, support your view with a high degree of credibility.*

2. *As much as 12 to 15 minutes of a network television show is occupied with short, compact persuasive presentations. They are called commercials. Some are very direct in making their call for change: Buy our deodorant to attract a sexual partner. Wear these shoes to improve the shape of your posterior. Save money at our store tomorrow. Use this lawyer to get money fast. Drink our beer, not theirs. Other commercials are more subtle in their approach, more indirect: If you buy this upscale model luxury car you will look good. When the time is right you should consider our product. The persuasion is still there, only less confrontational. To underline the importance of analyzing your audience, think about the commercials you found interesting. Odds are that the commercials you evaluated as effective are the ones that appealed to your needs. For example, you pay attention to refrigerator prices only when you need a refrigerator.*

NOTES

NOTES

NOTES

NOTES

NOTES